Book: (Read Aloud @ brain function)

Your fantastic elastic
Brain   Joann
Diek

Taking the PYP Forward

Edited by
Simon Davidson
and
Steven Carber

D1158762

John Catt Educational Ltd

First Published 2009

by John Catt Educational Ltd,
12 Deben Mill Business Centre, Old Maltings Approach,
Melton, Woodbridge IP12 1BL

Tel: 01394 389850 Fax: 01394 386893
Email: enquiries@johncatt.co.uk
Website: www.johncatt.com

ISBN: 978 1 904724 71 1

Set and designed by
John Catt Educational Limited

Printed and bound in Great Britain
by Bell & Bain, Glasgow, Scotland

Contents

Taking the PYP Forward

About the Editors

In 1997, **Simon Davidson** began working in international schools, starting with a small school in Brussels, and then moving to Zurich International School, which was one of the first schools to introduce the PYP. Simon then founded and led the International School of Como, Italy. He was also Primary Principal of Bonn International School, which he helped develop into one of the world's leading PYP schools. He is currently researching communities of inquiry and working as an educational consultant.

Dr Steven Carber teaches full time for Endicott College's MEd in International Education programs in Madrid, Leysin, and Prague. He has presented at international education conferences in Nairobi, Accra, and Mexico City, and has published several articles on international education and the PYP. He also works as an educational consultant, having served in this capacity in locales such as Sacramento and Palo Alto, CA. His PYP teaching dates back to the fourth-authorized PYP school in the world.

About the Authors

Jason Cone is currently the Head of IT Curriculum at Zurich International School. As the ZIS Lower School IT Curriculum Coordinator, he implemented an integrated IT curriculum at the Lower School, which has become a model school for IT in the PYP. Jason has presented at educational conferences on IT in the PYP based on Zurich International School's integrated approach. Jason holds a Masters degree in Educational Technology and a BSc in Biological Sciences and Education.

Sarah Craig is the Head of Junior School at Branksome Hall, an independent IB World school for girls in Toronto. Involved with the PYP since 1999, she was first introduced to the ISCP back in the mid-1990s when teaching in Morocco. As a PYP Coordinator, she led Upper Canada College through the authorization process and Branksome Hall through the evaluation process. She is an IB workshop leader and has visited many schools as a site visitor and consultant.

Greg Curtis is currently the Curriculum Director for the International School of Beijing. Prior to this, he worked for 11 years at a PYP school in Europe, serving both as Director of Curriculum and Professional Development and Director of Information Technology. He is a frequent presenter at conferences on topics ranging from technology infusion to all-school strategic planning. Greg's professional interests lie in the areas of curriculum design, technology infusion, curriculum mapping, futures-thinking for schools and internationalism.

Brian Dare is an education consultant who has worked across a range of international contexts in language and literacy and ESL. He has written and delivered a number of professional development courses which have a strong focus on the role of language in teaching and learning across the curriculum. He is one of the co-writers and accredited tutor trainers for the Teaching ESL Students in Mainstream Classrooms (TESMC) course, the ESL in the Mainstream for the Early Learner course and the Language and Literacy Course.

Marcella Emberger is a consultant and an ASCD faculty member, focusing on the improvement of teaching using research-proven methods, and the companion task of developing assessments that inform instruction. Her work involves all personnel in the education system from classroom teacher to administrator to central office supervisory staff. Her varied background serving in each of these capacities, and as a liaison among them, allows her to successfully work with all the members of the education community.

Rosemary Evans is the Academic Director at Branksome Hall, an independent school in Toronto. She has overseen the implementation process for the International Baccalaureate programmes at her school, including the Primary Years Programme, the Middle Years Programme and the Diploma Programme. She has presented on critical thinking, inquiry, assessment, and curriculum design. She taught in the pre-service program at the Ontario Institute for Studies in Education, and was the recipient of a teaching excellence award.

Dennison MacKinnon is the principal of The Codrington School, Barbados. He holds a teaching certificate with triple distinctions, a first class honours degree and a Master's degree from the University of Wales. He has previously worked as a teacher and administrator in Zambia, Wales, Sri Lanka, Greece, Germany and The Bahamas. Dennis has been involved with the PYP since 1991, when it was the ISCP, and chaired the project's steering committee at the time The ISCP was handed over to the IB in 1997 as the PYP.

Jay McTighe, educational author and consultant, draws on experiences developed during a rich and varied educational career. He is co-author, with Grant Wiggins, of the best-selling *Understanding by Design* series, including the newly-released *Schooling by Design* (2007) and *Connecting Content and Kids: Integrating Differentiation and Understanding by Design* (2006), co-authored with Carol Ann Tomlinson. Jay has an extensive background in staff development and is a regular speaker at national and international conferences and workshops.

Ken O'Connor is an independent consultant in classroom assessment who specializes in issues related to grading and reporting. Previously he was a high school teacher and a curriculum coordinator in a large school district in Ontario, Canada. He has written two books and contributed to others. Ken has presented at many conferences in Canada, USA and for NESA, AISA and EARCOS. He was born in Melbourne, Australia, but has now lived more of his life in Toronto.

Pam Oken-Wright MEd is a teacher-researcher, author, and consultant who has worked with five-year-olds at St Catherine's School in Richmond, Virginia, since 1979. She is a member of the Lugano research collaborative for the study of Reggio principles in US contexts and is on the editorial board of *Innovations in Early Childhood Education: The International Reggio Exchange*. She has contributed to a number of other publications about Reggio practice.

Dr Jeb Schenck is unique in education as both a practicing classroom teacher and memory researcher where he can see which theories actually work. He teaches high school biology, college biology, statistics, and graduate courses on how the brain learns at the University of Wyoming. Dr Schenck is the author of the forth-coming comprehensive work - *Implementing Neuroeducation: A Practical Guide for Educators* - to be published 2010.

Kathy G Short is a professor of Language, Reading and Culture at the University of Arizona and has worked extensively with teachers to develop curriculum that engages students as inquirers. She is the co-author of many books, including *Creating Classrooms for Authors and Inquirers, Learning Together through Inquiry,* and *Literature as a Way of Knowing*. She is the director of Worlds of Words, an initiative focused on encouraging dialogue around children's literature to build bridges across cultures.

Foreword

The International Baccalaureate Primary Years Programme (PYP) stands in a proud tradition of reflective educators incorporating best practice into international schools. It emerged from the International Schools Curriculum Project (ISCP) as a creative endeavour from teachers and administrators in international schools who thought deeply about contemporary best practice, and how to implement it in their settings. They developed a curricular structure that enables rich inquiry teaching, and which has made a huge contribution to education in international schools and beyond.

However, education doesn't stand still. Inquiry has to be rethought, refreshed and reapplied. Otherwise the PYP would present the leading ideas of the 1990s to 21st century schools, and gradually lose its relevance. Therefore it is important to circulate a broad range of thinking about inquiry education for PYP teachers, administrators and workshop leaders to draw upon. We hope that this book helps facilitate that process.

We have chosen to bring in voices from both within and outside of the PYP, recognising the importance of collaboration with the broader educational community. Therefore we have voices as diverse as Jay McTighe, Pam Oken-Wright, Jeb Schenck and Kathy Short. These voices broaden our view of inquiry and its relevance for all areas of learning, and enable us to take the PYP forward.

Some of these voices speak about the nature of inquiry (chapters 1 and 2). They describe assessment practices that have developed substantially since the early years of the PYP (chapter 4) and look at the importance of understanding (chapter 5). They talk about teaching English as an additional language within an inquiry framework (chapter 6) and provide inspiring examples of early childhood education from Reggio Emilia (chapter 10).

As well as fresh thinking, there are also many fresh challenges and opportunities. This can be seen in the diverse range of information technology available to educators, and the challenges for using it effectively (chapter 7). It can be seen in many new insights into the workings of the human brain (chapter 9), and the difficulties and successes schools can have with action in the PYP (chapter 8).

Increasing knowledge raises many questions about what to teach, and what to leave aside (chapter 3). Global mobility means that schools have to support the transitions of third culture kids, and often third culture teachers and parents too (chapter 11), and show the importance of internationalism for international and non-international schools alike (chapter 12). In such a complex situation, we have to look beyond traditional structures to understand quality (chapter 13).

Collaboration is also central to any significant project, and this book is no exception. First and foremost we would like to thank all the contributors for their writing, and for their patience with our editing as we coordinated across four continents. We also thank the IB legal department for their approval of the project, and the curricular office for their help and cooperation.

Mary Hayden from the University of Bath was also very helpful in connecting the editors with key people. Alice Sikora and Sara Goacher additionally gave great support and were wonderful sounding boards for ideas. We would like to thank Terry Haywood for his feedback and mentoring over the years. We have benefited tremendously from the inspiration and insights of great colleagues, including the staff of Bonn International School, Endicott College, and all those who read draft manuscripts or gave advice, including Paul Morris, Marina Gijzen and many others.

Simon Davidson and Steven Carber
February 2009

Chapter 1

Inquiry as a stance on curriculum

Kathy G Short, University of Arizona, USA

Inquiry is one of those frequently-used terms that educators rarely define because they assume a shared understanding. Most often, inquiry is used to signal that learners ask questions and engage in research, and so educators focus on getting students to ask better questions and to develop effective research strategies. Ironically, this view of inquiry often leads to teacher-directed projects and activities that are fun and engaging, but that actually violate the deep structures of inquiry. Inquiry is not a particular teaching method but a stance that underlies our approach to living as learners, both within and outside of school. Within schools, inquiry highlights learning as a process that underlies curriculum across disciplines, subject areas, and age levels. We have always known that *how* we teach influences students as much or more than *what* we teach. Inquiry immerses us in exploring the learning process and using those understandings to shape how we teach our content so that an inquiry stance on learning permeates our teaching.

Since curriculum involves putting a set of beliefs into practice, we need to examine and articulate our beliefs in order to explore ways of enacting those beliefs in classrooms with students.[1] Curriculum as inquiry thus involves exploring inquiry as a stance on learning and envisioning ways of bringing that stance to life in classrooms.

Inquiry as stance

My first response to inquiry was skepticism because experts often use new terms to label old concepts so their approaches seem fresh and new. I had explored theme units for some time and the talk about inquiry seemed, on the surface, like adding a stronger focus on research investigations to theme units, rather than something fundamentally different. The tensions I was experiencing about theme units, however, gave me pause and led me to explore the possibilities of inquiry within curriculum, although initially I saw inquiry as a method, not a stance.

As a student, I experienced *curriculum as fact* through a textbook curriculum that emphasized skills and facts with right answers and correct procedures for getting those answers. Teachers covered the content through textbooks, worksheets, tests, and research papers. We covered lots of topics and memorized many facts, to be forgotten as soon as the test was taken or the research paper handed in. We ended up with superficial knowledge and no desire to keep learning about a topic – an indication that these experiences were not educative.[2]

As a teacher, I wanted to make curriculum meaningful for students and so explored ways to actively engage students, such as writing workshops, literature circles, and theme units. This approach of *curriculum as activity* immersed students in a range of reading, writing, and research activities around particular topics. My tensions about these activities grew out of observations that the activities still involved covering the curriculum and facts, just in a more engaging way, so that, while I did not ask students to memorize facts, they still collected facts.

I often felt as though we were doing activities at the expense of critical, in-depth knowing. I was uneasy that the units remained teacher-driven since I was the one setting up the projects and activities within which students asked and pursued questions. The learning in these units was limited by my knowledge of the topic and students often viewed this learning as school-based, with little connection to their lives. The focus on topics like family, nutrition, or water made true curricular integration difficult – the activities were correlated across subject areas, but not integrated across the curriculum and students' lives in significant ways.

These tensions led to discussions with colleagues and to theorists such as Dewey, Freire, and Vygotsky to search for other ways of thinking about the construction of understanding. Several of us formed a study group where we worked together to enact *curriculum as inquiry* in our classrooms, meeting over several years to make sense of our experiences. We struggled with the difficulty of enacting our beliefs, challenged by students' responses to our attempts at inquiry. Our experiences convinced us that inquiry was not a refinement of project approaches or theme units, but a stance on learning that challenged our perspectives as teachers.[3]

The problem with defining inquiry is a stance is that describing a stance or philosophy is much more difficult than describing teaching methods or processes. I often find myself describing the different ways that inquiry might play out in classrooms, and avoiding defining the stance itself. Understanding and articulating inquiry as a stance, however, are essential to moving beyond projects and units to curriculum as inquiry. Changing a few engagements in our classrooms is much easier than changing our thinking about learning and that is what a stance of inquiry invites us to do as educators.[4]

For me, *inquiry is a collaborative process of connecting to and reaching beyond current understandings to explore tensions significant to learners.* Inquiry is a stance that combines uncertainty and invitation. A feeling of uncertainty encourages us to wonder and question, to move beyond current understandings to pursue new possibilities. Without invitation, however, we may not feel the courage to pursue those uncertainties or tensions; invitation beckons us to feel some safety in taking the risk to pursue those possibilities by thinking with others.

Inquiry is thus a reaching stance of going beyond information and experience to seek an explanation, to ask *why* and to consider *what if*. Lindfors[5] argues that inquiry involves going beyond in intellectual, social, and personal ways – we go beyond our current understandings, our sense of identity, and our engagements with others. This process of going beyond is dependent on remaining connected to current understandings as the point from which to reach out and requires the support of a collaborative community. We need to know that we are still connected to the known and are not totally separated from the ideas and beliefs that ground our lives. At the same time, if we do not reach beyond, we get stuck in a rut. Thinking with others provides the impetus and zone of safety from which to reach out.

Inquiry is also a stance of being off-balance. Although the self-help literature trumpets the need to lead a balanced life, a state of perfect balance involves staying perfectly still in the same place – in that comfortable rut. Reaching out occurs because learners experience a sense of being off balance or in tension, the driving force that compels learners to move forward (Dewey, 1938). Tension disrupts a learner's sense of unity and understandings about life, and this disruption compels learners to pursue a tension to reach toward new insights and unities.

Inquiry is natural to learning

A particular set of beliefs about learning underlies inquiry as a collaborative process of connecting to, and reaching beyond, current understandings to explore tensions significant to the learner. The first is that inquiry is natural to how children and adults learn outside of school contexts. In fact, I would argue that three-year-olds epitomize inquiry: they engage with life, immersed in what is occurring around them until something catches their attention and raises curiosity or doubt.

This curiosity creates a need to know that they explore through play and observation and through pestering adults with questions. They move from curiosity to knowledge that leads to more in-depth investigations (unless something more compelling catches their attention). These explorations and investigations, in turn, support them in constructing their understandings of the world and in asking new, more complex, questions.

Inquiry invites us as educators to base instruction on the processes that are natural to learning – to investigate how people learn and build curriculum from these processes. The typical approach is to create instruction based on how we think people should learn, to ask "How do I teach inquiry?" instead of first asking, "How do I and others inquire?" Once we explore inquiry as natural to learning, then we can engage in the difficult task of creating learning environments that immerse learners in these processes, rather than in how we think they should learn.

Barnes[6] argues that many students operate as if there are two boxes of knowledge in their heads – an action knowledge box that contains the knowledge used to function in their daily lives and a school knowledge box that contains what is learned in school. They close the action box as they enter the classroom, assuming that knowledge is irrelevant in school, and open the school box, reversing the process at the end of the day. A stance on inquiry invites students to function with action knowledge both inside and outside of school.

Inquiry is based in connection

Inquiry has no other place to begin than in learners' own experiences and current understandings. Bateson[7] states that learning is the search for and finding of patterns that connect. Without significant points of connection, learning remains difficult and easily forgotten because that learning is experienced as isolated ideas and information. This search for connection distinguishes tension that drives learning from stress that shuts down the learner.

We typically begin a unit by teaching new information and covering key points about the topic to provide students with a knowledge base. Inquiry starts with immersing students in engagements so they can find and connect to their life experiences and so we as teachers can observe and listen to students' current understandings. Connecting in significant ways to students' lives means we often have to move beyond the topic so that, for example, a unit on immigration might begin with students exploring their experiences of moving from place to place, rather than with information on immigration patterns within a particular part of the world.

Inquiry is conceptual

If our goal is only for students to gain information on particular topics, then a curriculum based in inquiry is not essential. Inquiry includes but goes beyond information to search for an explanation, to understand the why behind that information. Inquiry is a conceptually-based, rather than a topic-based, approach to curriculum. Conceptually-based curriculum puts the major emphasis on the big ideas that lie behind topics, leading to deep essential understandings that transfer across contexts.[8]

Information and knowledge are still significant, but the goal is no longer to cover a particular set of information, but instead to build the knowledge necessary for providing the base from which to explore conceptual understandings that underlie that knowledge. Knowledge becomes a tool to explore conceptual understanding rather than an end in and of itself.

Preparing students for the 21st century has become a frequent topic in education, based on the assumption that we have moved from an Information Age that depends on knowledge workers and analytical thinkers, to a Conceptual Age depending on the ability to combine creativity and analysis.[9] Children and adults need to be able to think conceptually in order to identify the critical issues of our society – to not be distracted by the massive flow of information around them – and to be able to apply their understandings and knowledge in future contexts that have not even begun to unfold in the present.

The focus on topics and content, however, is so deep-rooted in how we think about instruction that the conceptual frame for units of inquiry is easily lost. A unit on water may begin conceptually around the central idea of the consequences of the limited availability of natural resources, but get lost in information about water shortages and water conservation.

Or a unit on nutrition may be framed conceptually around making choices that affect our health and lives but get lost in information on body systems, bones, and food groups. A conceptual frame focuses on the biggest idea behind the central idea – to the very essence of the unit, such as choice or limited availability – so that our attention remains on the 'why' of that unit.

These experiences have forced me to realize that units of inquiry need to begin with connection to the conceptual frame, not to the topic, as the essence of that central idea plays out in children's lives. Water is the topic and limited availability is the concept, so the connection is the consequences of limited availability in students' lives, not to water but to whatever they might currently experience as a limited resource. Nutrition is the topic and choice is the conceptual frame, so the connection is to the choices children make in their lives in comparison to the decisions that adults make for them.

A group of first grade teachers planning a unit of inquiry on endangered animals realized that they needed to start by exploring a conceptual understanding of loss, not with information about animals. They invited children to tell stories about losing things (a very common experience for six-year-olds) to understand the feeling of losing something forever in contrast to the joy of finding something they thought was lost. This conceptual frame provided a different perspective for children from which to consider the possibility of losing animals that are endangered in our world.

Many units of inquiry are designed to build initial knowledge separate from the conceptual frame with the goal of gradually working toward conceptual understanding; the result is that students focus on information in isolation from that frame. If inquiry is conceptual, then that frame must be the first focus of attention and be woven throughout the unit, not a conclusion we hope students might reach. The topic is a case study, a way to get at the broader conceptual understandings, not the actual focus or rationale for that unit of inquiry. As teachers, we are so used to covering content that we lose sight of the conceptual frame and immerse ourselves in designing activities to cover the content, to teach water or nutrition or endangered animals.

Inquiry is problem-posing and problem-solving

One of the most common understandings of inquiry is problem-solving with the vision of students engaged in research on particular topics of interest related to the class focus. The teacher sets up a situation to pose an engaging problem as a means of encouraging students to ask questions about that problem and to research those questions. A common approach to science, for example, is to provide students with batteries, wires and bulbs, and ask them to determine what causes an electric current to light the bulbs. Students are encouraged to ask lots of questions but the problem itself is already determined. Teachers often plan a unit to result in research projects around a focus already determined before the unit even begins, such as deciding that children will research the systems of government, family and education for particular ancient civilizations, or break into groups to research a specific explorer.

These experiences of guided inquiry provide students with strategies for how to go about research, but they do not learn how to find a problem that matters and is worth investigating in the first place. Scientists undertake investigations because they have a problem to solve. Inquiry begins with exploring a phenomenon of interest and attending to problems or tensions that emerge and that are worth taking the time to investigate. Scientists also have to be able to develop experiments that will further that investigation. We short-circuit the process by handing students the experiment and asking them to engage in the procedures of science labs, but not the processes of scientific reasoning. They do not actually experience science.

Freire[10] argues that the person who poses the problem is the one who remains in control of learning. Inquiry makes us nervous as teachers because we may feel as though we are turning over control to our students. By retaining our role as problem-posers, we keep control, while at the same time seeming to actively engage students as inquirers. The problem is that they are asking questions about the problems we have posed, not the issues significant in their lives. They never fully experience inquiry.

Students need to know how, out of everything that is possible to know or experience, to determine what is significant and worth pursuing. It is essential that learners know how to reason through a question or problem to investigate it, but problem-solving is not sufficient. We do not want students to become problem-solvers who only pursue the questions that others pose for them and do not question the questions.

Many curricular models of inquiry start with students asking questions as the first step and then delineate in detail the steps to investigating those questions. My experiences as a researcher show that finding the question is often the most difficult part of the inquiry process and that often the question does not emerge until the study is almost over.

As a researcher, I start with a particular interest or tension, and then spend time immersed in the context, gaining knowledge through observation, conversation, and professional reading. The question or problem that is worth investigating grows out of knowledge and experience with the research focus. Even when I start with a particular question, that question usually changes once I know more. Problem-posing is not a simple starting point for a researcher; it is a process that goes across the research, intertwined with and informing the problem-solving.

Asking students what they know and what they want to know (KWL) at the beginning of a unit of inquiry may provide insights into current understandings, but not for posing problems. Frank Smith[11] argues that you can't think critically about something you don't know anything about. Posing thoughtful questions grows out of knowledge about a topic or issue and that takes time and immersion in explorations to see what tensions develop and become compelling for learners.

Although we may be able to predict those tensions, we cannot determine what will cause a specific learner to feel tension. Dewey[12] argues that the role of the teacher is to create a learning environment that has the most *potential* for creating anomaly or tension for learners. Learners need voice and knowledge to determine what is compelling for them to pose as a problem worth investigating.

This distinction between problem-posing and problem-solving distinguishes between guided inquiry, personal inquiry, and collaborative inquiry. Personal inquiry involves the learner as both the problem-poser and problem-solver in pursuing personal interests and tensions that may never be the focus of the school curriculum. Independent reading, writing workshops, and expert projects are examples of engagements that can provide the space for students to pursue inquiries growing out of personal interests or life issues.

Collaborative inquiries, where teachers and students collaborate on problem-posing and problem-solving through a process of negotiation within the curriculum, are at the heart of units of inquiry. Teachers influence the problems that are posed through engaging students with specific materials and experiences as well as by determining the understandings at the center of a particular unit of inquiry. Teachers, however, negotiate the curriculum *with* students, not just build curriculum *from* students, so that investigations grow out of process.

Guided inquiry, where the teacher is the problem-poser and students are problem-solvers, is often found in skill instruction. For example, teachers may use assessment to determine students' needs as readers and form a guided reading group to work on a specific reading strategy. Within the group, the teacher poses the problem that is the focus of the group and engages students in a meaningful reading of a text, within which they actively engage in reasoning to develop their own understandings of that strategy.

The tension for teachers is providing the space within classrooms for students to move in and across personal, guided, and collaborative inquiries. The project-based approaches that many schools have taken to inquiry are problematic only because all of their engagements and units are guided inquiries and students never experience posing problems. The units are filled with interesting projects and activities and end with summary projects that involve students in problem-solving to demonstrate their understandings. What gets left out is time for students to pose and investigate problems they find compelling within that unit.

Inquiry is collaborative

Since inquiry involves reaching beyond ourselves and our current understandings, we need collaborators with whom we can think to challenge us to outgrow ourselves. Those collaborators may be real (members of our immediate community with whom we talk and interact) as well as virtual (authors with whom we think in books or on internet sites). Schools often focus on cooperation, dividing up a task into different roles for students to complete. Inquiry goes beyond cooperation to collaboration where students think together, not just work together, through dialogue about ideas. Freire[13] argues that this dialogue is how we transform ourselves as human beings.

Vygotsky's[14] Zone of Proximal Development provides another rationale for the necessity of learning *with* others. Vygotsky argues that the most conducive space for learning is defined by what can be learned with the support of collaborative others. This space is located between the point of what learners can already do independently and the point at which they can only function if someone takes over the task for them.

Lave and Wenger[15] argue that the most effective learning occurs within communities of practice where members work together toward understanding. These communities of practice involve participating in activity, not listening to someone, so that members learn in experience, not just *from* experience. Inquiry takes place in participation, not in individual minds. It is a way of being *in* the social world, not just coming to know *about* that world.

Everyone actively participates as a member of that community; while some may be less proficient or are newcomers with limited participation, they are still members of the community. For example, all children are viewed as English language learners with some more proficient in their use of the language, but no one is a non-speaker positioned outside of the community.

We construct understanding by working collaboratively with others, who are more or less expert, on problems that arise out of practice and are focused on understanding and improving practice within that community. Teachers may thus be at the center of the community in terms of their expertise and knowledge, but students are members of the community and have the responsibility of thinking collaboratively with their teachers and peers. Students are collaborators, not just informants, and so actively engage with teachers in negotiating curriculum.

Enacting inquiry in the classroom

Moving from these beliefs about inquiry to practice in classrooms is facilitated by the use of a curriculum framework. A framework provides a guide for planning curriculum based in theory as well as a structure for connecting theory and practice that reflects the complexity of the process. Curriculum frameworks provide a bridge between theory and practice that supports teachers in more consistently enacting theories. We are able to teach in a theoretically consistent manner because the framework allows us to articulate what is most significant. A framework provides the bigger picture, particularly highlighting the relationships between the parts, so that we can more effectively work at those parts within the whole.

Inquiry as a stance involves a set of beliefs about the learning process that can be depicted in a range of curricular frameworks. Although there is no one 'correct' framework, the framework I use to plan and implement curriculum based on my beliefs about inquiry as a process of learning, is the Inquiry Cycle.[16] The inquiry cycle is an authoring process in the sense that learners engage in authoring or constructing meaning about themselves and the world. A unit of inquiry on human rights with ten- to 12-year-old students in Tucson, Arizona, provides one example of how this framework might play out in a classroom.

Figure 1. Inquiry Cycle

The Inquiry Cycle

Kathy G. Short & Jerome C. Harste, 2002

Connection

The inquiry cycle does have a specific starting point within any unit of study and that is with connections to the life experiences and understandings of learners. Connection gets at the *why* rather than the *what* of a unit. This connection to the broader conceptual frame involves getting at the essence of the central idea that frames a unit, for example the big idea of making choices as the why behind a nutrition unit. The role of the teacher is to immerse students in engagements, so they can explore their current understandings of the conceptual frame for the inquiry, by considering how that idea is already present and significant in children's lives.

In the human rights inquiry, our conceptual focus was on 'rights' as the needs we have as human beings in order to live in a society. We knew that children would struggle with the difference between 'needs' and 'wants' as well as the balance of 'individual voice' with 'group responsibility'. In reflecting on rights, we realized that this idea plays out in students' lives in their complaints about what is unfair, especially at lunch or recess. We read aloud *A Fine, Fine School*[17] to begin our conversations about unfair decisions in school and put out many picture books about school for students to browse. Students created unfair maps of their school on which they labeled places where unfair events had occurred.

Once the maps were completed, we talked about what determines when something is unfair, and that the feeling of unfairness is often based in a sense of rights being violated in some way. Students worked in small groups to create lists of their rights within the school, based on the entries on their unfair maps. These discussions were intense and engaged, providing them with a conceptual understanding of rights as well as strong connections to their own experiences.

Invitation

Students are invited to expand their knowledge, experiences, and perspectives in order to go beyond their current understandings. Teachers immerse students in a range of engagements, that encourage their active exploration of the inquiry focus and increase their knowledge through providing access to resources and experiences. Invitations often take the form of guided inquiry, in that the teacher has determined particular lines of inquiry related to the unit focus, that are significant for students to gain a strong depth and range of knowledge about that focus.

In offering invitations, we found that it's important to be selective and to remember that the emphasis is not on covering the inquiry focus, but on expanding knowledge to build understanding and raise tension. There are always many interesting and worthwhile activities and projects to consider; engaging students in all of these takes over the entire unit, leaving no time for in-depth investigation. The key is to select the most significant lines of inquiry *as connected to the conceptual frame*, instead of covering the content; for example, choosing engagements that highlight making choices that affect our health, not covering nutrition.

Another consideration is to choose engagements that actively involve students, such as text sets or exploration centers, where they have time to explore and observe as well as have the opportunity to make choices and engage in conversation. These engagements should start closest to the students rather than at the farthest historical point. A unit in which students compare systems of government, family, and school in ancient civilizations to their own lives, for example, may be more effective if the engagements start with their lives and then move back in time.

Also, while informational books and websites are important resources, powerful pieces of fiction, including both novels and picture books, are significant in moving students from information to conceptual issues. The careful choice of a chapter book to read aloud as students engage in these explorations, can keep the focus on the conceptual frame, helping to prevent students becoming lost in gathering information.

In the Human Rights inquiry, we immersed students in read alouds and text sets to expand their knowledge of human rights to the global context. We put out text sets containing fiction and non-fiction picture books, and newspaper articles around issues such as child labor, discrimination, freedom/government, violence, basic needs, education, and the environment.

Students had time to read from these books as well as to talk with each other and web the issues that were emerging. We also read aloud and discussed picture books such as *The Carpet Boy's Gift*,[18] a story based on child labor in carpet mills in Pakistan. Student interest in the boy who led a movement against this practice led to choosing *Iqbal*[19] as a chapter book read aloud. Students struggled with judging parents who sell their children to work in these mills and in understanding the tremendous poverty that led to such a difficult decision.

Tension

As students expand their understanding about the inquiry focus, tensions emerge that are significant and compelling and that they want to pursue in greater depth. These tensions may be expressed as wonderings or issues, not questions. They signal a shift from information, fact-based questions to issues that students find compelling and from teacher-guided inquiry to student-driven inquiry. In order to know when this shift has occurred, some system of keeping track of students' wonderings and issues needs to be in place in the classroom throughout invitations, such as individual 'I Wonder' journals or class charts that are added to on a daily basis through reflection on particular invitations.   Wonder Wall

In the human rights inquiry, we regularly gathered for reflection after read alouds or text set browsing for students to share their observations and add to a chart of issues about human rights. In addition, after reading for several weeks in the text sets, students worked in small groups to web their understandings and tensions about human rights.

Our initial plan had been to see what area of human rights emerged as a strong interest and move into investigations around that area, looking both locally and globally. We were surprised to find, however, that the most compelling issue for students was how kids can be involved in taking action. They had not believed that they could make a difference as kids and much of their discussion focused on the strategies that Iqbal and other children, in books, were using to take action for social change.

At that point our focus shifted to taking action on violations of rights and we realized that taking action in their own school context was most compelling to them. They cared about the ways human rights were playing out in global contexts but they needed to experience taking action in their own context. Also, they did not have enough in-depth knowledge about particular global issues to take action in thoughtful ways. They were clearly still at an exploration stage with these issues, but ready to investigate how to take action in the school.

To highlight strategies for taking action, we engaged in several dramas around books in which children took action on social issues, in particular homeless people and undocumented immigrants from Mexico. In these dramas, they took on the roles of characters from within these stories and interviewed each other in pairs, with a reporter asking a character questions about the action that child took within the story.

Investigation

Investigation is a shift to problem-solving and in-depth investigation on a particular issue or question, with students often working as partners or in small groups to support each other through dialogue and research. Their focus is unpacking complexity, not developing simple solutions to complex problems. The teacher's role involves a major shift because the nature of these investigations cannot be determined ahead of time if they truly reflect the tensions that are significant for students.

If several classes are engaged in the same unit of inquiry, this is also the point where those classes *should* look different from each other since the focus is on what is compelling for students. If the classrooms look the same during investigations, that is a strong signal of teacher-guided projects rather than collaborative inquiry. These differences will also be evident within a classroom across students with different tensions that they want to pursue.

Teachers play a key role in planning structures for supporting students in organizing their investigations but not in determining their focus. One of those roles is helping students create plans for their investigations by reflecting on questions: Why are we interested in this issue? What are our related questions? What do we really want to know? What will we do to investigate our question? What is our plan for investigation? What materials and resources do we need to gather to implement our plan?

Students in the human rights inquiry returned to their unfair school maps and webbed the problems they still saw as significant within their school context. Their original webs of problems were somewhat self-serving, without consideration of how their desires would affect other students. We hoped that when students returned to their maps after the global exploration of human rights and taking action, they might have a different understanding of the balance between individual needs and responsibility to the group.

This shift was evident in that issues the students had raised earlier that would benefit a few at the expense of others, such as specific playground rules or when to do classroom work, were no longer raised. Each small group chose the top one or two problems from their list to share with the class and each class engaged in a discussion to determine, through consensus, the problem they wanted to take on as a class. They talked about their experiences with that problem and brainstormed a list of people who had perspectives on the issue. They then invited several to come to the classroom for an interview with the whole class. They also individually conducted other interviews. Based on these interviews, they came to a consensus on a strategy for taking action.

Both classrooms involved in this study focused on taking action about a school issue because the same tension was evident; however, their webs of problems and the problem they decided to focus on differed. They decided to come to a consensus on one problem as a class, instead of breaking into small groups on different problems, because they recognized the difficulty of taking action with adults in school contexts. One group was concerned about the quality and options for school lunches, particularly the lack of fresh vegetables and fruit. After interviews with school personnel, they found out that their lunches were made in a central district location and then trucked to schools. They realized that the problem was district-based and worked on a petition (that they asked parents, children and teachers to sign) for delivery to the district head of food services and the superintendent.

The other class was concerned with their lack of voice in decisions about the many rules that governed their play on the playground. Upon interviewing their parents, they realized that there was a tremendous difference of opinion and reasons for and against why children should have a voice in school rules. Their interviews with playground monitors gave them insights into why adults made rules, who was making the rules, the haphazard nature of how rules were created in response to a situation, and differences between older and younger students' views of the rules.

Demonstration

During investigation, the role of the teacher shifts from offering invitations based on the lines of inquiry to supporting student investigations through demonstrations that respond to students' needs. Demonstrations offer students possibilities for what they might do, rather than modeling what they must do. These demonstrations are often research strategies or tools, such as note taking, internet searches, or skimming to locate information. In the human rights inquiry, demonstrations included developing questions and taking notes in interviews.

Re-vision

As students engage in inquiry, they need opportunities throughout the process to pull back and reflect on their learning. Our minds seek unity and investigation upsets that unity as we attend to difference, to what is new or unlike from what we already know. Students need to continuously reflect and make sense of what they are learning, not the information, but on connections between these ideas and their thinking – they create a new unity or vision of the understandings that guide their inquiry.

This re-vision can be encouraged by an ongoing learning log or other device for reflecting on learning. In our case, we used small group and whole group webs as well as class reflections at the end of research sessions to engage in this re-visioning of understanding.

Representation

Inquiry is never-ending; there are always new questions and issues to pursue. At some point, however, learners pull together their learning and go public with what they have learned. While not final, these public representations support them in recognizing how much they have learned as well as what they still need to know.

These representations take a variety of forms as appropriate to particular investigations, such as reports, skits, murals, and posters. Often that form varies from group to group within a classroom. In one classroom in the human rights inquiry, the representation took the form of signed petitions and a formal letter that were sent to the district food services director and superintendent.

In the other classroom, students developed a proposal for a committee with several students from each grade level, who would meet with the principal and playground monitors once a month to review new rules and issues on the playground. The students spent a great deal of time developing structures for who would be on this committee, and when the committee could meet, as well as how students could become advisors to the adults on rules affecting children in the school.

Valuation

Representing what has been learned to an audience opens an opportunity for learners to pull back even further to reflect on what is of value from their learning for themselves and the world. They consider their learning of content, process, and intentions/goals to determine the value of this learning for future inquiries and to reposition themselves in the world. In our case, students brainstormed a class web of what taking action meant to them conceptually, as well as created individual sketches in which they symbolically depicted the meaning of taking action. This summative assessment connected to the central idea and conceptual frame for the unit.

One common misconception is that the summative assessment should be a major project that addresses the lines of inquiry and so the time needed for investigation is taken over by summative assessment. Instead of student-driven inquiry, students engage in another guided inquiry. The summative assessment focuses on the broad conceptual frame of the unit, the central idea, and can be a reflective engagement that does not require large amounts of time.

Action

Any research needs to address the 'So what?' question of the kind of action that is now possible, given the investigation. What difference does this study make in the broader context of the inquirer and the world? The learner has gained new understandings from this inquiry, but what action will now be taken because of those understandings? What are the new questions or tensions to pursue based on these understandings? If action is not addressed, then the artificial separation of action knowledge from school knowledge is continued.[20]

In our case, the action was built into the investigation in that the representations involved taking action in the school setting. The issue of thoughtful ways of including students' voices in adult considerations of school decisions was one that continued to be raised across a range of contexts within the school across the year and was the source of continued action.

Conclusion

Inquiry is not merely a 'new' set of instructional practices, but a theoretical shift in how we view curriculum, students, learning and teaching. Inquiry as a stance influences how we teach and create learning environments for students. More importantly, however, a stance of inquiry influences who learners become as human beings.

Indigenous educators argue that the difference between western and indigenous perspectives is that western societies emphasize *schooling* students to become good *citizens* while indigenous societies emphasize *educating* students to become good *human beings*.[21] Inquiry as a stance brings together these perspectives to argue that we have a responsibility to help students to become good citizens *and* good human beings – to develop wisdom as well as knowledge. Inquiry transforms education from learning *about* to learning to *be* – to the process of becoming.

References

1. Short, K. G., and Burke, C. (1996): Examining our beliefs and practices through inquiry, in *Language Arts*, 73, pp23-30.

2. Dewey, J. (1938): *Experience and Education*. New York: Collier.

3. Short, K. G., Schroeder, J., Laird, J., Kauffman, G., Ferguson, M., and Crawford, K.M. (1996): *Learning Together Through Inquiry: From Columbus to Integrated Curriculum*. York, ME: Stenhouse.

4. Short, K. G., and Burke, C. (1996): Examining our beliefs and practices through inquiry, in *Language Arts*, 73, pp23-30.

5. Lindfors, J. (1999): *Children's inquiry*. New York: Teachers College Press.

6. Barnes, D. (1976): *From communication to curriculum*. London: Penguin Press. 1st Edition.

7. Bateson, G. (1980): *Mind and nature*. New York: Bantam.

8. Erickson, H. L. (2002): *Concept-based curriculum and instruction*. Thousand Oaks, CA: Corwin; (and) Wiggins, G., and McTighe, J. (2005): *Understanding by design*, 2nd Ed. New York: ASCD.

9. Pink, D. (2005): *A whole new mind: Why right-brainers will rule the future*. New York: Berkley.

10. Freire, P. (1978): *Pedagogy of the oppressed*. New York: Continuum.

11. Smith, F. (1983): *Essays into literacy*. Portsmouth, NH: Heinemann.

12. Dewey, J. (1938): *Experience and Education*. New York: Collier.

13. Freire, P. (1978): *Pedagogy of the oppressed*. New York: Continuum.

14. Vygotsky, L. (1978): *Mind in society*. Cambridge, MA: Harvard University Press.

15. Lave, J., and Wenger, E. (1991): *Situated learning*. London: Cambridge University Press.

16. Short, K., Harste, J. and Burke, C. (1995): *Creating classrooms for authors and inquirers*. Portsmouth, NH: Heinemann. 2nd Edition.

17. Creech, S. (2001): *A fine, fine school*. New York: HarperCollins.

18. Shea, P. (2003): *The carpet boy's gift*. Gardiner, ME: Tilbury House.

19. D'Adamo, F. (2001): *Iqbal*. New York: Aladdin.

20. Barnes, D. (1976): *From communication to curriculum*. London: Penguin Press. 1st Edition.

21. Cajete, G. (1994): *Look to the mountain: An ecology of indigenous education*. Albuquerque, NM: Kivaki Press.

Chapter 2

Communities of inquiry

Simon Davidson

The International Baccalaureate's Primary Years Programme (PYP) is an inquiry-based programme. However there are many definitions and facets to inquiry, and many layers to the PYP. It can be hard to see their connections and relate them to the actual processes of learning. Therefore I investigated some of these aspects, and how they combine in PYP classrooms.

I looked at inquiry as a creative process; a community pursuit of new understanding by applying, adapting and recombining different concepts and skills. As such, the process requires and develops a set of powerful ways of thinking, the *tools of inquiry*. These tools are given meaning and purpose by the social and intellectual life of the class.

I first considered these tools of inquiry. As a cultural species, we have many tool systems to master.[1] In didactic teaching, they form the core of traditional subject-based learning. In inquiry they are building blocks that will be integrated and used creatively to understand complex ideas. Some of these are *physical tools*, like pencils and computers. Others are *psychological tools*: a broad range of mental constructs and processes as diverse as addition, note taking, and the scientific process.

Children also learn to use a variety of *languages and sign systems*, such as the many different forms of English or Chinese; or the languages of various domains such as music, visual representation or mathematics. As they learn these tools, students acquire a range of *component skills*,[2] overcome misconceptions, and learn the ways of thinking of different disciplines. As in didactic learning, much of this happens through processes of internalisation, in which social activities become part of students' individual mental functioning.

The greatest differences between inquiry learning and didactic teaching are not in the tools themselves, but in how the class functions as a community to develop and use these tools in the pursuit of new insights. Several social aspects are involved: the classroom community is underpinned by shared purposes and values; there are shared classroom routines and approaches; there are shared ways of talking that support the main purposes; the students have varied and changing roles and relationships. It is useful to think of these community aspects of learning as processes of transformation.[3]

These elements together give a multi-dimensional model of inquiry that spans the life of the class, which develops into a Community of Inquiry at the beginning of the year, and develop as a community over the year. As a community, students and teachers explore complex areas, by applying tools from 'stand alone' units and from 'frontloading' in the creative pursuit of enlightenment. They move between sign systems in processes of *transmediation* and combine powerful ways of thinking to understand the complexities of today's world.

An inquiry-based programme

The PYP is an inquiry-based programme.

> At the heart of the Primary Years Programme's philosophy is a commitment to structured inquiry as the leading vehicle for learning.[4]

Rather than a definition, inquiry has many elements throughout the PYP. The word 'inquiry' pervades PYP documentation. Approximately half of a student's time in school is spent investigating 'Units of Inquiry'. The PYP seeks to develop students as inquirers in that:

> They develop their natural curiosity. They acquire the skills necessary to conduct inquiry and research and show independence in learning. They actively enjoy learning and this love of learning will be sustained throughout their lives.[5]

PYP inquiry includes students asking deep questions and exchanging knowledge with peers, mastering 'inquiry skills' and subject concepts. They learn to organise and plan. It accommodates 'a wide variety of teaching strategies and styles ... provided that they are *driven by a spirit of inquiry* and a clear sense of purpose'.[6] It is clearly complex:

> Inquiry involves an active engagement with the environment in an effort to make sense of the world, and consequent reflection on the connections between the experiences encountered and the information gathered. Inquiry involves the synthesis, analysis and manipulation of knowledge, whether through play for early childhood students (three to five years) or through more formally structured learning in the rest of the primary years.

Inquiry can be an all-embracing approach, more significant than a methodology or set of procedures. In fact, according to Jerome Harste, inquiry is more of a philosophy and a frame of reference, and 'a metaphor for the lives we want to live and the people we want to be'.[7]

As well as a philosophy, the PYP has several layers, many of which have an abstract quality. It has a deep set of values embodied in the IB Learner Profile: inquirers; knowledgeable; thinkers; communicators; principled; open-minded; caring; risk-takers; balanced; and reflective.

The PYP has five 'essential elements': it is structured around eight *concepts*: form; function; causation; change; connection; perspective; responsibility; and reflection. It has a set of *transdisciplinary skills*: social skills; communication skills; thinking skills; research skills; and self-management skills. Students should learn *knowledge* across the traditional subject areas: language; mathematics; social studies; science; personal, social and physical education; and the arts. It encourages a specific set of *attitudes*: appreciation; commitment; confidence; cooperation; creativity; curiosity; empathy; enthusiasm; independence; integrity; respect and tolerance. There is an *action* cycle of choosing, acting and reflecting.

Students study six *transdisciplinary themes*: who we are; where we are in place and time; how we express ourselves; how the world works; how we organise ourselves; and sharing the planet. It uses a sophisticated planning process, with several stages laid out in the PYP planner. It includes summative and formative assessments, and a system of portfolios. Its view of learning is 'transdisciplinary', but it acknowledges the need for sufficient coverage of the traditional subjects.

This gives a complex set of layers, concepts and vocabulary that can be hard to combine. Yet the exact nature of learning through inquiry beneath all these layers has not yet been pinned down. This may have advantages in avoiding losing some of the richness of inquiry. However, the result can be vagueness and different partial meanings for different people. It is possible to get lost in all the layers, or have difficulties seeing how these elements actually combine in the classroom. Teachers can initially find the PYP confusing, and different teachers understand it differently.

Such complexity, rather than adding richness, can lead to opting for a simpler reduced version of inquiry, for example as a question-asking and information-finding process. It may change the source of facts, while students continue to memorise them, and teachers still organise the process.[8] Many parents find it difficult to understand how their children are learning. Children can think that asking a question and inquiry are the same thing. It can be hard to see the inquiry for the proverbial trees. To overcome this, one has to make inquiry and its learning processes visible. We need a more robust view of inquiry.

Developing tools

The first part of a more robust view is to have a clear understanding of how students develop the tools of inquiry. Humans are a species of tool users. As we grow up, we gain our language, ways of thinking and ways of living from those around us. However, some tools need extensive development to pass on, so schools provide a forum where children can learn what has worked in the past. Some of these involve using physical tools: children learn to use pencils, protractors, calculators and maps.

Perhaps more significant, however, are psychological tools,[9] the various powerful concepts and notions and the different symbolic systems that children learn. These can be such notions as numbers, memory techniques, algebraic symbolism, language, works of art, writing, diagrams, maps and conventional signs. They can be mental versions of rulers, graphs, brainstorming, or teacher questions. They can be a broad range of sign systems. Like spoken language, music, dance and mathematics have their own vocabulary and grammar. Our world is made of symbols and meaning.[10] Such tools provide children with multiple ways of knowing and different potentials for meaning.

Human nature is not just about preserving the tools of the past. We develop and modify existing tool systems constantly and develop new ones. Other primates also have aspects of culture, but humans are unique in that we 'accumulate modifications over time, that is to say, we have cultural histories'.[11] The ways we think are based on 'cumulative cultural evolution'. That's why our culture is different from that of 500, or even 100 years ago. Over the centuries, societies have developed powerful ways of thinking, which may be very different from communities in other places or times. As new challenges appear, we respond to them by technological and cultural innovations.

Therefore, as well as passing on tools, we want students to be able to develop them. Education is only partly about learning one's cultural inheritance. It is also about enabling students to learn from the past and, as Isaac Newton said, stand on the shoulders of giants. Over the centuries, as more and more tools have accumulated, schools have organised their transmission to subsequent generations in increasingly systematic ways. However, transmission models do not develop our capacities for creation and modification of tools. In inquiry classrooms these aspects can be given much greater emphasis.

Subject disciplines

In spite of the power of combining domains in communities of inquiry, disciplines themselves have a key importance. They have a proven success over history that students can tap into, which we don't want to lose in our urge to combine them. We want our students to become experts in each discipline. This has some important aspects to bear in mind.

Phil Phenix noted that each discipline has representative ideas that generate new knowledge in the field whilst being useful to novices:

Representative ideas are clearly of great importance in economizing learning effort. If there are certain characteristics of a discipline that represent it, then a thorough understanding of these ideas is equivalent to a knowledge of the entire discipline. If knowledge within a discipline is organized according to certain patterns, then a full comprehension of those patterns goes far toward making intelligible the host of particular elements that fit into the designs of the subject.[12]

Students need to become familiar with these ideas, so it is useful if they are included in the scope and sequence for each subject. This provides a set of 'disciplinary lenses' that students can use as 'tools and toys for inquiry'.[13] They form and test hypotheses as scientists. They use graphs to represent and analyse data like statisticians. They approach the past as historians.

Unfortunately, although these overarching ideas are powerful and highly flexible, they are not the whole story. Each discipline also has a wide assortment of component skills, which may be highly compartmentalised, and take many years to master.[14]

Research on component skills has found much of them to be very specific. For example, Giyoo Hatano found that children's use of the abacus was highly compartmentalised, and learning didn't transfer to other number activities such as pencil and paper tests.[15] As children master writing, with all its breadth and flexibility, there are discrete components to master such as phonic awareness and handwriting. These smaller components are not an end in themselves, but are important enablers for the higher order formats and purposes like persuasive writing and narrative that have significant cultural value beyond school.

One has to be careful about what can be considered transdisciplinary, as many specific skills need specific development. They can, however, be applied across many contexts with the tools of other disciplines.

Misconceptions

Students have another challenge as they master disciplinary tools. They come to class with many misconceptions – naive understandings that only work in limited circumstances and require major change. Howard Gardner showed that even many graduates have retained naive misconceptions, and although they have other 'schooled' concepts, they continue to apply naive views in many situations. They don't have a deep connected level of understanding.[16]

Schools have traditionally been good at *adding* facts that enrich their native theories, but less successful in ensuring significant *change* to their individual underlying theories. As we look to provide students with powerful tools of inquiry that they can apply outside limited boundaries, it can be helpful to consider *bottom up* and *top down* learning.[17]

In bottom up learning, ideas are generally added unconsciously, based on experience. This may be the predominant mechanism in general culture and 'lay thought'. It can also be useful in the classroom, as students gain experience of an area and get a 'feel' for what should happen. For example they may watch plants growing and notice how they become bigger and that sometimes they die. They might draw from these experiences that plants, like animals, feed, grow, and die, and develop broad notions of living things. They may be able to draw analogies from their experience to new situations. With appropriate experience they may undergo *spontaneous conceptual change*. However, misconceptions can also form and remain unchallenged.

Schools have commonly also had top down instruction, in which students are presented with activities, presentations and demonstrations that allow children to understand a pre-defined model.[18] When done well, children understand the models and apply them well in classroom exercises. However, top down learning doesn't necessarily connect or confront their existing ideas. Students may add new concepts whilst preserving their previous ones, or they may concoct an inconsistent hybrid model with inconsistencies that are not examined in the classroom. Profound conceptual change takes time, and learning has to address students' previous conceptions.

Fortunately, the extended nature of PYP units of inquiry provides a great vehicle for doing so. When frontloading at the beginning of a unit, students can spend time in observation and familiarisation with the area being studied. This provides a good opportunity for bottom up learning and to draw out their intuitive theories based on everyday experience and lay culture.

Well-crafted teacher questions and activities can provide provocations to think situations through and introduce top down models. Discussion can ensure that students have an explicit knowledge of their own beliefs so that inconsistencies surface, more robust understandings develop, and concepts are changed rather than new ideas being added. Note that all students have to think through their ideas, not just agree as a group. As Hatano said, "It is unlikely that conceptual change is induced only by social consensus."[19]

Learning in the PYP is further complicated by key concepts that in themselves do not reveal misconceptions in different domains. Students may have a concept of historical *change*, and still have misconceptions about scientific *change*. They may have understood aspect of *causation* from forces in a simple machines unit, but have a very naive view of *causation* in history.

Internalisation

Many individual aspects of learning can be understood as *internalisation*. Individual thinking is said to exist first in an external social plane, and then become individual mental tools, part of the child's individual mental functions. These tools are 'formed as individuals engage in practical social activities'.[20] They can then be applied in different contexts. As such, internalisation is useful to describe psychological tools and component skills such as decoding text and adding numbers. When you can decode a particular word, you can decode it in any context.

This would be similar in good non-inquiry teaching. Students should leave inquiry classes with the skills and concepts that they would have gained in didactic teaching. For example, they have the mechanics of reading and writing, and of performing arithmetical calculations. They can use maps, and have a knowledge of science and social studies.

However, this model does not account for situations in which thinking and acting remain as social activities, or are integrated into the 'social plane' of the classroom community or other social situations. Consider jazz musicians improvising.[21] They have certainly mastered, or internalised, the techniques and language of jazz. They also interact with each other and create something new, because the final purpose for jazz musicianship is not individual, but social.

When students learn to read, they not only acquire a broad range of abilities, but also become part of a community of readers, and interact around books.[22] They enter a new social world of stories, characters and ideas. Their social plane transforms into another social plane.

Developing as a classroom community

As humans, we are not independent and autonomous. We live and work with others, and use our learning as part of a community. Cultural tools are given their purpose and meaning from the community around them. This is where inquiry learning comes into its own.

Inquiry classrooms are, like any classroom, a particular kind of community. They form at the beginning of the school year, and develop over the course of the year. However, whereas many features of didactic classrooms are based around organisation separate from the content that is being learned, many social aspects of the inquiry classroom are organised around the pursuit of understanding. They are not just collections of students following a curriculum, but a community of inquiry.

To investigate this further, I have heavily adapted several features of Communities of Practice from Lave and Wenger[23] to represent PYP classroom communities. As a community, a class has shared purposes and values; shared classroom routine and activities; shared talk; and changing roles.

Shared purposes and values

A community isn't just people who happen to be together. They come together for a common purpose. In school this is primarily learning, although the social nature of school is very significant, and children often want to come to school also to see friends.

At the beginning of the year, the teacher sets out values. Some may be personal or school ideals. Others are common to PYP schools, such as the values of the IB learner profile, PYP attitudes, and an international outlook. In inquiry classrooms, many aspects are also discussed and negotiated so that shared values emerge. Cultural values therefore partially reflect the cultures and personalities of the students, so that classes are different from year to year. The importance and shared nature of these values are often reinforced by displaying them around the classroom.

As the year goes on, the values develop and some purposes change as the class matures and focuses on new units. As different units of inquiry start, their central idea and teacher questions are usually also displayed to demonstrate their importance as the classroom community's shared purpose.

Shared classroom routines and activities

The class also establishes, develops and draws from a broad repertoire of behaviours, activities and routines. Some of these are organised by the school schedule. There are recess and lunch arrangements. Students typically go to single subject teachers for scheduled classes such as music, art, physical education and languages, which provide an additional set of activities.

Other routines are not academic, but based on other aspects of community life, such as distributing newsletters and end of day routines for tidying the classroom.

Shared responsibility for these aspects of the classroom, is an important part of the class as a community that can help develop shared responsibility for learning. There may be other routines to develop tools systematically, like daily reading practice, which are similar to other forms of education, both in their form and purpose. Other routines reflect PYP values, such as reflection, so that classes will typically have arrangements where they regularly talk through their learning together or write about it in a reflection journal.

In addition to the set routine of the classroom, classes develop a repertoire of activities that they become familiar with and skilled at using, and can be drawn on as appropriate. For example, they brainstorm or review ideas as a class, moderated by the teacher, who often scribes what is said. They may work individually for a period of time, either at their desk, or spread around the classroom.

They are likely to become familiar with a structured writing process, such as peer planning, drafting, reviewing in groups, editing and then finally sharing or displaying their work. Many classrooms have routines around creating research posters, where students become familiar with agreed formats for finding, organising, analysing and displaying information from a variety of sources. They may have procedures for science experiments and art activities.

It takes time and energy to establish all these routines and activities at the beginning of the year. However, when they are embedded in the class as a shared repertoire, much of the responsibility for their maintenance can gradually be shared with the students, and energy can be devoted to refining them and adding additional patterns of learning.

Shared talk

Some of the most important practices are around classroom talk, which serves many purposes. Some talk is conversational chat, which is important in sustaining relationships – an important part of any community. However, my focus here is how talk is used in a shared pursuit of understanding.

A common misconception for those new to inquiry-based approaches is that inquiry talk is about asking questions, phrased as questions. This can lead to the situation Lindfors describes[24] where students develop a routine for listing questions, not because of genuine doubts and curiosity, but because it is part of a teacher-pleasing questioning routine they have mastered. This is not true inquiry. Like a game of 20 questions, or guessing what the teacher is thinking, it is an entertaining activity where some skills are learnt. However, there is little search for understanding complex issues.

Non-inquiry questions also form an important part of teacher discourse. A tell-tale sign is when teachers already have a clear answer for questions they ask. Often such questions are in IRF form,[25] when the teacher has an *initiation*, the students give a *response*, and there is *feedback*. For example:

Initiation: What is the capital of France?

Response: Paris.

Feedback: Well done!

The teacher clearly asked a question, but it was not an act of inquiry. The teacher is not seeking knowledge for its own sake, or extending thinking, but looking for short closed answers.

Students are familiar with this format and may well frame their first questions similarly. In a habitats unit they may ask, "What is the fastest/most dangerous animal?" In a landforms unit they may ask, "What is the biggest mountain?" These could be good 'factoids' but they don't address the complex systems being investigated in true inquiry. (Don't say "What an inquirer!" when a student asks such questions.)

Inquiry addresses more significant issues than can be phrased in questions with simple answers. It involves more complex exploration that may centre on a more complex question, or investigate ideas that are not phrased as questions at all. Rather than having a particular grammatical form, inquiry involves ambiguity, doubt and multiple perspectives. It may not start with a question, but with organising your ideas and thinking through what you want to know.

Inquiry classes have many ways besides questions of talking to develop understanding. As with activities, a class develops a repertoire of ways of talking and agreed ways of using them, what Mercer calls *ground rules*.[26] These typically include a wide variety of formats and activities such as class discussion involving turn-taking and listening; persuasive talk and debates; students formulating and articulating hypotheses with a partner, a group or the whole class; teacher explanation; paired sharing, planning or reflection; open brainstorming sessions; individual and group prepared presentations.

In inquiry these are combined in a long conversation[27] that connects a wide variety of tools, concepts and activities to the inquiries and purposes of the classroom. Often there is some form of discussion between every activity, relating them to the larger inquiries behind them.

In many PYP classes, the need for students to justify their thoughts is central to the ground rules for all these activities. Teachers may regularly ask questions like "Why do you say that?" or "How do you know?" Unlike IRF exchanges, the answer is not a closed reply, but an account of the student's reasoning. Children may often contradict themselves or change their opinions. Skilled inquiry teachers are careful not to point this out directly, but to allow children to notice this in themselves and each other, so that the community becomes the intellectual control. After a period of time students need less prompting, requiring perhaps only a glance to elicit an account of their reasoning. Eventually students justify aspects of their thinking to many members of the community, not just teachers, as a matter of habit.

There is also a high quantity of reflection with feedback on learning in inquiry classrooms. Like assessment, it has ongoing and summative aspects, and like good assessment, it is a shared community process, with the teacher the main 'expert', but with students increasingly involved as they learn to share responsibility. There are *micro-level* reflections and feedback concerning reformulating remarks, elaborating and correcting errors, and *macro-level* reflections and feedback that review and adjust the direction of the inquiry. Units typically also end with summative reflection discussions.

Student roles

Students in inquiry classes adopt a wide variety of roles. They may dominate discussions or listen. They may plan and organise, keep groups on task, or distract their peers. They may play the role of a writer, or be a critical friend to a peer. Roles may vary widely between students with different personalities and from different cultures. Students, like members of any other community, are not all the same. Some ask more persistent questions, others like to learn many small facts. Some are very competitive and others are more concerned with relationship and harmony. Some come from cultures that value outgoing behaviour, whilst others come from cultures where children are expected to listen quietly.

In community, provided there is cohesion, such diversity is a great strength. Students learn to cooperate and appreciate each other, their personalities, strengths and weaknesses – values worth cultivating for life. Thus they learn how the whole can be more than the sum of the parts, how sharing, as well as pooling valuable contributions from different people, makes the contributions themselves better. This gives students a great experience of the strengths of collaboration and diversity that they would not receive in more individually-based approaches.

That doesn't mean that there is no place left for traditional student roles in the inquiry classroom, or that the role of being a student is too 'inauthentic'. On the contrary, it is very authentic to learn to be a good learner. Students still need to be able to concentrate and complete tasks independently. The routines of inquiry classrooms may be different than traditional classrooms, but students still need to learn to follow them, and allow other students to follow them undisturbed when necessary.

Schools have a valuable role in the transformation of children into strong learners and community members. This is an especially important role and dramatic transformation in early childhood classes. Perhaps some school roles are not the final destination of education, but they may be necessary for the journey, in PYP schools and in other schools that students may transfer to.

Experts

Students don't only learn to play particular roles in specific activities. They can also learn to be 'experts' in particular areas, and to take the roles of 'experts' in different disciplines.

Some students become a 'go to person' in the class, an 'expert' in a particular skill set or area of knowledge that matches their interests or abilities. This is a valuable experience, as they begin to know what it is like to develop specialist knowledge or skills – even if it is just about bugs. They can learn to develop this expertise as part of their identity, and feel the satisfaction of a certain level of age-appropriate mastery, and of contributing this to the class community. As children assume the identity of an expert, their confidence develops, sustaining individual learning. They are also better prepared for later success in interdisciplinary teams, as they know how to be a specialist who works with others.

As well as personal expertise, all students can benefit from learning the role of disciplines. As well as the particular ways of thinking mentioned above, students can learn to see themselves as scientists, artists, writers and so on. They can say, "I am being a scientist. My perspective is...", or "I am being a geographer. I know about maps. I will draw a plan to show us what the island looks like". They might consciously take the role of a mathematician in an inquiry as they perform necessary calculations, or be a reporter who records what students are thinking or feeling. Thus children get used to playing many roles and developing expertise.

The exact roles may neither correspond to traditional disciplines, nor map easily onto curricular scope and sequences, but they have clear identities and require sets of expertise with different component skills, many of which are important educational goals. Students, like adults, may develop component skills much better when they see themselves as experts in the area.

There is another range of expertise around the life of the community that is significant to communities of inquiry. They develop all the abilities needed to work with others to develop new understanding. These are partially reflected in transdisciplinary skills: the social skills; communication skills; thinking skills; research skills; and self-management skills.

Of course the key expert in the class is the teacher, who will have significant expertise across the main aspects of classroom life. Teachers are master writers, master planners, master mathematicians and so on. Some may even also be master artists or musicians. Students can observe how they apply such expertise to inquiry, especially when teachers can also share the inquiry, and allow themselves to be uncertain of its outcomes, and curious about what will emerge. That is one advantage to units with challenging central ideas, so that there is room for inquiry from even skilled and knowledgeable adults.

As students interact with teachers as expert inquirers, they can gradually assume the characteristics of such a role. They too become master storytellers and master organisers, and mutual supporters who give each other guidance, feedback and encouragement.

Participation

Such community learning does not match up well with the internalisation model, because students' roles, purposes and activities always keep a social dimension. Therefore they are better described using a *participation* model[28] in which learning is described by how these social dimensions change – a 'transformation of participation'.

The participation model also provides the concept of *legitimate peripheral participation* (LPP)[29] to describe how new members join a community. Initially they participate in simple risk tasks that are nonetheless productive and necessary to fulfill purpose. Through peripheral activities, they become familiar with tasks, vocabulary, and roles of the community.

Students new to a class often watch quietly at the periphery, particularly if they aren't familiar with some aspects of the classroom. Very young children may be unfamiliar with school. Many students in international schools arrive with little English. Some have only been in traditional schools, and don't recognise the ground rules of inquiry classes. Their participation on the periphery can be legitimate! They can start to engage with the class community in roles that they are familiar with, and gradually this participation transforms into 'core participation'. They will know how to perform core roles because they have connected with them from the margins. If newcomers are separated from the 'experts' they will have limited experience and understanding of how to be a strong inquiry learner.

One of the key core community members that all students observe and interact with is the teacher. Teachers can facilitate students' observations of their 'expert practices' by pointing out and explaining the salient features, so that they understand the broader context into which their own efforts fit. When they are familiar with roles, even if they haven't done them directly, they are able to take the roles when needed.

With so many dimensions to a group of children becoming a community of inquiry, setting them up at the beginning of the year is an involved process. However it is powerful for developing educated ways of thinking, acting and relating that the children will use all year long and beyond. It can be particularly useful to begin the year with units that explore community processes. For example units that explore rights and responsibilities, friendship or conflict resolution can all be used to explore and develop the effectiveness of the classroom as a community.

Putting the elements together

Inquiry learning is unique, not just for the community processes in the classroom, but in how it uses these processes with all the tools and sign systems that students have available to them to discover new ideas and solutions. This unleashes students' creative potential and allows them to develop rich understandings of complex phenomena. Students can be absorbed by this creativity, and experience the pleasures and rewards of what Csikszentmihalyi called *Flow*.[30]

In more static periods of history, with a stable culture and knowledge base, transmission could be sufficient for most of society, with perhaps a minority involved in knowledge creation. Students could succeed by the acquisition of ideas organised previously by others, and developing a closed range of skills. They could succeed in schools by learning what was on a pre-defined syllabus and reproducing it on tests. Creativity could be limited to specific exercises, perhaps in some forms of writing and the arts, and then disappear from much of students' lives. Inquiry may not be the most appropriate form of education for such situations.

Currently, however, we live in a complex, changing and interconnected world. We face many complex situations that don't all have straightforward solutions. To prepare our students to face these challenges, they still need the transmission of previous knowledge, but also to be able to constantly rethink and apply learning in new ways. They also have to be able to develop new solutions that will be complex and creative. It increasingly means developing projects in teams across disciplines.

PYP units address this by providing even very young students with complex contexts that can only be resolved by applying multiple tools and sign systems, and by collaboration. Such an approach can become a disposition, a habit of mind.

Transmediation

PYP units don't only use different disciplinary tools separately. When students examine the same area through several different lenses, there is a process of *transmediation*[31] that produces a new and deeper understanding. Students make new connections through representing thought in different sign systems.

A complex Central Idea is explored using different disciplines, and is possibly emphasised differently in different Teacher Questions. Ideas move from one domain to another. Children may make posters combining texts and images, representing ideas they found in other formats. They act out situations from written accounts, or write about information from maps and diagrams. They make an oral presentation on what they read, or present a written report on what they have seen and heard. They might carry out an experiment, and draw about their hypothesis of the processes behind it. As they transfer their ideas, students have to think deeply. As they do so, they produce new meanings and develop richer and stronger understandings. As Short and Kauffman said:

> This is not a simple transfer or translation of meanings from one system to another because the meaning potentials in each system differ. Instead, learners transform their understandings through inventing a connection so that the content of one sign system is mapped onto the expression plane of another.[32]

Effective transmediation can be simple and short. Pause for a few minutes to draw a picture. Act something out. Swap talking for writing. Take a break from individual writing to explaining your ideas to others. It isn't always their comments that help, but the process of talking, of using another medium.

Transmediation shows the real power of a transdisciplinary approach. It is at its most powerful when students exchange ideas with others, respecting different skills, personalities, cultures and perspectives.

Conclusion

The PYP has a complex curricular model, with many more layers than traditional curricula. However, by investigating how students learn tools, and in how they work as part of a community of inquiry to apply, develop, and combine the tools, we can understand and improve many of these layers. We can then have a robust view of inquiry.

Inquiry isn't just a convenient or fun methodology. When done right it addresses the core of human nature and the needs of contemporary society. As we move from a manufacturing economy to a knowledge-based economy, today's global citizens need to be able to combine and recombine a broad range or tools of inquiry, develop new ones, and adapt to whatever new situations may be around them. They have to exchange and develop knowledge with others. Communities of inquiry can prepare students to do so.

Students then develop a broad range of individual abilities and social capabilities. They gain the most important elements that traditional education also develops. They learn the same tools as before, to become powerful disciplinary thinkers who are fluent in many sign systems.

In addition, they learn to face unfamiliar situations with success. They learn to be part of a creative intellectual and social community. They can move beyond existing knowledge, exchanging ideas with others, combining, adding, reconfiguring, and applying knowledge to the unfamiliar. They learn to approach complex problems and relish challenges, becoming creative inquirers with a love of learning. Perhaps this is more important than any individual tool, because when they know how to learn and work with others, they will be able to master any additional tools that they need later. They will be well prepared for the challenges of the 21st century.

References

1. Rogoff, B. (2003): *The cultural nature of human development.* New York: Oxford University Press.

2. Cole, M. (2007): Giyoo Hatano's Analysis of Psychological Tools, in *Human Development*, 2007, 50, p78.

3. Lave, J., and Wenger, E. (1991): *Situated Learning: legitimate peripheral participation.* Cambridge: Cambridge University Press, p51.

4. International Baccalaureate Organisation (2002): *School's Guide to The Primary Years Programme.* Geneva: IBO, p6.

5. International Baccalaureate Organisation (2002): *IB Learner Profile Booklet.* Geneva: IBO, p5.

6. International Baccalaureate Organisation (2007): *Making the PYP Happen.* Geneva: IBO, p30.

7. Harste, J. (2001): What Education as Inquiry Is and Isn't, in Boran, S., and Comber, B. (eds): *Critiquing Whole Language and Classroom Inquiry*. Urbana, IL: National Council of Teachers of English, p1.

8. Short, K., *et al: Learning Together Through Inquiry: From Columbus to Integrated Curriculum*. Portland: Stenhouse Publishers, p23.

9. Kozulin, A. (1998): *Psychological Tools*. Cambridge: Harvard University Press.

10. Deacon, T. (1998):*The Symbolic Species*. New York: Norton.

11. Tomasello, M. (1999): *The Cultural Origins of Human Cognition*. Cambridge: Harvard University Press, p40.

12. Phenix, P. (1964): *Realms of Meaning*. New York: McGraw-Hill. p323.

13. Harste, J. (2001): What Education as Inquiry Is and Isn't, in Boran, S., and Comber, B. (eds): *Critiquing Whole Language and Classroom Inquiry*. Urbana, IL: National Council of Teachers of English, p5.

14. Howard Gardner estimates ten years, not including primary education, in many of his books.

15. Hatano, G. (1997): Learning arithmetic with an abacus, in Nunes, T., and Bryant, P. (Eds.): *Learning and teaching mathematics: An international perspective.*(pp.209–232). Hove: Psychology Press.

16. Gardner, H. (1991): *The Unschooled Mind: How Children Think and How Schools Should Teach*. New York: Basic Books.

17. Vosniadou, S. (2007): Conceptual Change and Education, in *Human Development*, 2007, 50, pp47-54.

18. *ibid.* p47.

19. Hatano, G., and Inagaki, K. (1994): Young children's naive theory of biology, in *Cognition*, 50, p195.

20. Ratner, C. (1997): *Cultural Psychology and Qualitative Methodology: Theoretical and Empirical Considerations*. New York: Plenium Press, p97.

21. This example is drawn from Matusov, E.: When Solo Activity Is Not Privileged: Participation and Internalisation Models of Development, in *Human Development* 1998, 41, pp326-349.

22. Smith, F. (1992): *Learning to read: The never-ending debate*. Phi Delta Kappan, February, pp432-441.

23. Lave, J., and Wenger, E. (1991): *Situated Learning. Legitimate Peripheral Participation*. Cambridge: Cambridge University Press.

24. Lindfors, J. (1999): *Children's Inquiry: Using Language to Make Sense of the World*. New York: Teachers College Press.

25. Mercer, N., (1995): *The Guided Construction of Knowledge*. Clevedon, Multilingual Matters, p29.

26. Edwards, D., and Mercer, N. (1987): *Common Knowledge: The Development of Understanding in the Classroom*. London: Routledge.

27. Mercer, N., (1995): *Guided Construction of Knowledge*. Clevedon, Multilingual Matters, pp70-71.

28. Wenger, E. (1999): *Communities of Practice: Learning, Meaning, and Identity*. Cambridge: Cambridge University Press.

29. Lave, J., and Wenger, E. (1991): *Situated Learning: Legitimate peripheral participation.* Cambridge: Cambridge University Press.

30. Csikszentmihalyi, M. (1990): *Flow: The Psychology of Optimal Experience.* New York: HarperCollins.

31. Siegel, M. (1995): More than words: The Generative Power of Transmediation for Learning, in the *Canadian Journal of Education*, 20, pp455-475.

32. Short, K., and Kauffman, G. (2000): Exploring Sign Systems Within an Inquiry System, in Gallego, M., and Hollingsworth, S. (Eds): *What Counts as Literacy. Challenging the School Standard.* Columbia: Columbia University Teachers College Press, p43.

Chapter 3

What should students learn?

Steven Carber

The Saber-Tooth Curriculum
- Fish-grabbing-with-the-bare-hands
- Woolly-horse-clubbing
- Saber-tooth-tiger-scaring-with-fire

Benjamin, H R W (1939)[1]

'And above all, let them remember that the meaning of life is to build a life as if it were a work of art. In the end, the Basic School is committed to building lives as if they were works of art.'

Ernest Boyer (1995)[2]

Imagine, if you can, a scenario in which a parent asks a teacher or administrator about a perception that a child is missing some important content within their PYP experience: "Have you covered the topic of Spanish missions at all in grades 2-5? In our home region, this is one of the mandated standards for grade 4. I am worried that she will fare poorly on local tests when we return home in a year." How are PYP educators to respond, if they clearly know they have not implemented a unit on Spanish missions in any grade at the school in Geneva?

Here is a brief attempt at an answer, before we get deeper into this chapter: "We need to give Sarah a core set of 'new basics'[3] which the kids need, such as, for example, reading properly, research skills and knowing how to learn. If Sarah and her classmates can do these things, they may not know about the mission at Soledad, but they can find out about it quite easily. They will understand core concepts, habits of mind, and disciplinary approaches from which they can build mental 'scaffolds' to comprehend the significance of the Spanish presence in the New World or whatever the topic may be."

Before expanding upon this answer, though, let us look more closely at the nature of the problem.

Articulating the problem

There is too much to teach. Furthermore, international school students will move to new countries and states and in each will face new curriculum demands, some of them very content-heavy. The world they face contains so much to understand. Furthermore we are only recently realizing the need for emotional understanding and intelligence, and it would probably not be excessive to spend the majority of our classroom time, if we could, on managing positive relationships. We can't cover it all.

Limited space in the program of inquiry

Imagine a situation where all human knowledge and skill, those millions of items that fall into an exponentially growing list of topics and sub-topics in the information age, needed to be condensed into only 36 themes. You could choose only 36 – no more – and you would be lucky if you really got to all of those. Add in some separate lessons in mathematics, music and other specialist classes, and so on, and you still don't have a lot of space for learning. A school's program of inquiry generally encompasses only science and social studies-based units.

As challenging as that situation may sound, that is essentially the task that presents itself to PYP schools around the world, and indeed in some form, to all elementary schools everywhere whether PYP or not. If a student begins the PYP in kindergarten and continues until fifth grade, that comprises six years, with six units of inquiry to be investigated in each. A few readers may have heard tales of grade levels that only get around to covering five units annually.

In considering the problem of 'fitting it all in' we might notice our tendencies to focus too much on 'topics'. Recently, a school staff was debating the limited content of a program of inquiry, and one teacher, drawing on the work of Daniel Goleman,[4] said she'd like to see "managing positive relationships" added to the curriculum.

Realizing that being a manager of positive relationships was a *skill* as much as a topic, she suggested adding it to the school's learner profile, which of course opened up a different question: which list of adjectives really constitutes 'the ultimate' student profile? PYP schools make a commitment to the IB Learner Profile. Indeed, 'managing positive relationships' is probably not really a *topic*, and furthermore an emphasis on *topics* is limiting. Educators can find opportunities beyond the written curriculum and the program of inquiry to address skills like managing positive relationships.

Informing our response

The educator in the hypothetical example in the opening paragraph wanted students to understand core concepts, habits of mind, and disciplinary approaches from which to comprehend the significance of various specific topics not covered in class. The PYP educator is aware that, every year, the students have learned to interact with the PYP Transdisciplinary Themes, which has granted these children powerful habits of thinking, and these enable them to address all or most of the complex issues that they may have to learn about in the future.

International school students need a *portable education* – they have what they need when they go back to wherever they go to do whatever they need to do or to learn whatever they need to learn. Within the acquisition of this portable education, the transdisciplinary skills come into play, such as, but not limited to, research skills, organizational skills, communication skills, and ability to read well. Given the high order of reading tasks in the PYP and in student-generated inquiry, reading should be paramount in a PYP school.

Since we can't possibly learn all the 'bits', we should recognize that there are key *ways of thinking* and *ways of being* that are culturally important. These include elements of creativity; elements of critical thinking and problem-solving; treating others with civility; managing positive relationships; being able to self-assess whether one truly understands something, with a perception of what true understanding really is.

To further expand the notion of a portable education: Sam didn't know about, say, Celtic chieftains. He was an inquirer and articulated a genuine student question about their characteristics. He reflected and framed research questions about it and set goals. He searched and read good information about it, took good notes, and was organized. Shortly he understood what he needed.

Teachers have a role in this sort of process in that, to give Sam the needed abilities and transdiciplinary skills, we have to implement the PYP well, so that he has the deeper understanding with less content, and when he has the deeper understanding, he can quickly add in extra bits of information as needed. Parents also have a role in all of this during the transition process of moving, when students should take these skills back to their home country. Parents can bring along needed materials and can research expectations in a new land. The above is, in part, a portable education.

Literature-based responses to the dilemmas

What *should* children learn? What does literature suggest? Twenty years ago, Wiggins introduced relevant themes eloquently:

> 'The aim of precollegiate education is not to eliminate ignorance. The view that everything of importance can be thoughtfully learned by the 12th grade – notice I did not say "taught" – is a delusion. Those who would treat schooling as designed to educate students on all important subjects are doomed to encounter the futility that faced Sisyphus: the boulder of "essential content" can only come thundering down the (growing) hill of knowledge.'[5]

Wiggins' subsequent work with McTighe[6] played a key role in disseminating the notion that *understanding* was a more desirable goal than *coverage*. They articulated understanding in terms of six facets: explanation; interpretation; application; perspectives; empathy; and self-knowledge (reflection and metacognition).[7] The Understanding by Design work reminded us as well of the importance of big ideas and certain frames of mind within the disciplines, as articulated by Phenix:

> 'Representative ideas are clearly of great importance in economizing learning effort. If there are certain characteristic concepts of a discipline that represent it, then a thorough understanding of these ideas is equivalent to a knowledge of the entire discipline. If knowledge within a discipline is organized according to certain patterns, then a full comprehension of these patterns goes far towards making intelligible the host of particular elements that fit into the design of the subject.'[8]

As early as 1859, Herbert Spencer addressed the guiding question of this chapter, and claimed that the following hierarchy would indicate topics of greatest worth:

'Those that minister directly to self preservation, those that secure for one the necessities of life, those that help in the rearing and disciplining of offspring, those involved in maintaining one's political and social relations, those that fill up the leisure part of life and gratify taste and feeling.'[9]

But some of the 'necessities of life' change, as illustrated by the archaic nature of the Saber-Tooth Curriculum, summarized in the header for this chapter, from the famous satirical publication of 1939.

Broudy offered a thoughtful follow-up to Spencer's thoughts, noting that even though we forget many of the facts and skills that we are exposed to, 'we think and feel with the images and concepts that we have encountered in our school studies... It is of worth not because it has the approval of the social elites and not because it will have a direct occupational payoff [but] because this kind of context-building knowledge gives form to everything we do and think and feel...'[10]

Marzano's book *What Works in Schools* (2003) notes that K-12 schooling would have to be extended to something ridiculous like grade 22 or higher in order to even hope to 'cover' all that was mandated in the state standards of many US states.[11] Marzano and Ainsworth propose a solution within *Power Standards*, which this author interprets somewhat light-heartedly as the 'really *important*-important' things from those state standards lists; they have been carefully identified in part by looking at what is actually tested on standardized tests.[12] Wiggins' 1989 ideas seem even more 'reductionist' than the notion of Power Standards.

The emerging answer might lie somewhere in the overlap between Wiggins, Phenix, Broudy, Ainsworth, and Marzano. In considering these and related ideas, we may at least alleviate some anxiety about not getting around to covering the Spanish Missions, Rivers of the World, or whatever it might be this semester.

A complex set of issues

Schools which work on refining a program of inquiry over six elementary school years will realize that some elements should actually be spiraling 'throughlines', or maybe themes explored within other themes, rather than treated as 'topics' themselves.

For example, the scientific method will likely be more valuable when reviewed over and over during six years rather than taught as a 'unit'. Other throughlines might include the idea that myths express truth, the notion of limited resources in unlimited demand, and the concept of human expression through the arts. Project Zero and Teaching for Understanding endorse the use of throughlines, and they may have coined the term.[13]

Teaching for Understanding suggests that throughlines are 'overarching goals [which] describe the most important understandings that students should develop during an entire course'.[14] In the sense that I have used the term above, they may be understandings that spiral and should develop *during an entire six years of schooling*; this relates to the discussion below about the PYP transdisciplinary themes.

Framework to curriculum

When teachers engage in the process of determining six annual topics to be covered in their setting and grade, they are creating curriculum – they are moving the PYP from the level of framework and *the how* to the level of *the what*. This process may seem more spacious if they realize that there are actually *three* types of curricula experienced in the average school day: Eisner noted the explicit, implicit, and null curricula.[15]

Teachers may well realize that they are creating explicit curricula – those things that might be published on the school's or grade level's website, those things like planners that might appear in writing in 'giant binders' somewhere in the school. The explicit curriculum is generally synonymous with the school's written curriculum documents, which these days often appear online.

However, there is actually 'time' in which other things may be covered – the implicit curriculum is articulated by Eisner as what schools teach 'because schools are the kinds of places they are'.[16] Many of the things which we desire our students to learn, such as the notion of being managers of positive relationships, for example, can occur during the gaps between explicit instruction. Mind the gaps!

Treating each other with civility may be learned on the playground; as recess and lunch and trips to the water fountain are indeed parts of the implicit curriculum. The null curriculum, then, is that which is left out of schooling, be it how to buy stocks on margin or the history of certain nations.[17] Teachers can't avoid some things becoming 'null', but it is healthy to discuss that notion on a regular basis during planning.

The transdisciplinary themes

In *The Basic School*,[18] Boyer treated the question of what students should learn, and he offered a response that may have been on the minds of the ISCP teams when they created the six organizing themes. Boyer originally suggested eight core human commonalities; in the PYP one encounters six organizing themes containing somewhat similar notions.

When thematic instruction first became popular in education settings around the world, students might have participated in a unit about 'the color blue' or 'the circus' and so forth, but these in some cases may have lacked academic rigor and importance. When curricula spiral around notions like Boyer's human commonalities or the PYP's transdisciplinary themes, teachers have greater confidence of relevance. Boyer articulated the core commonalities in these terms:

1. All of us experience the cycles of life.

2. All of us seek meaning and purpose.

3. All of us develop symbols.

4. All of us respond to the aesthetic.

5. All of us have the capacity to recall the past and anticipate the future.

6. All of us develop some form of social bonding.

7. All of us are connected to the ecology of the planet.

8. All of us produce and consume.[19]

The perceptive reader will notice the parallels and the differences between the above and the six PYP transdisciplinary themes:

Who we are.

How we express ourselves.

Where we are in place and time.

How we organize ourselves.

Sharing the planet, and

How the world works.

We may breathe a sigh of relief that the PYP does not have us cover eight themes annually, but only six.

Boyer's and the PYP's lists drive as those sort of 'archetypal' elements that are important to all human beings on the planet and that resonate deeply within our psychology and around our sociological and political interactions. Elsewhere I have borrowed and adapted the term 'archetypal' from depth psychology to help drive at the notion of concepts or ideas or topics that resonate importantly with all human beings on the planet, whether Akha hill tribe members in Thailand, families in Ghana, or students in an international school in Berlin.[20]

The term as used here is not identical to its use in Jungian psychology, but similarly, it hints at powerful images and ideas that are part of our shared humanity, and that resonate with people in a variety of settings. Does that mean we should cover the archetypal story of Cinderella? Well, maybe, but the point is that the question 'Does this resonate deeply with all human beings on the planet?' could guide our program of inquiry and could help us frame central ideas.

The 21 Californian Spanish Missions may be of great interest and importance to students living in California, but the concepts of human migration and change may lead us to a better, non-case-specific central idea. Do the notions of human migration and colonization resonate importantly with all beings on the planet? What about the Akha hill tribe members? That is the type of question that might be applied in the very difficult weeding out process. (A peril in this process is to mistakenly assume that any given aboriginal community necessarily needs to or wants to know various 'western' constructs.)

To bring this down to the level of practical classroom talk, even if a group of teachers are not certain that they have chosen the 'ultimate' themes to address in a program of inquiry, if whatever they have created spirals around the PYP Organizing Themes, then they have an indication of being on target.

Regardless of whether one reads Eisner, Boyer, or Gardner and Perkins,[21] the importance of the fine arts comes up again and again in discussing what students should learn. Indeed, 'How we express ourselves' could perhaps be one of the most important of the six PYP organizing themes, and perhaps it could be seen as a throughline within all units of inquiry, rather than being treated as something that we address just once a year in one of our six units (not to suggest that the latter is what PYP schools are doing).

We would hope that students are producing meaningful works of art and music on a daily basis, and that they are learning to appreciate and respond to that of their peers. Could the incorporation of 'How we express ourselves' as some sort of a year-long throughline lead to five less-rushed units of inquiry per year rather than six? Or would this further reductionism be limiting in other ways? This is a topic for future debate; this chapter does not propose to have an answer.

The Transdisciplinary Themes, in a flexible manner, do address what students should learn, at least in large part. Among other things, they might help shift instruction from whole-language era *thematic* instruction to PYP-style *inquiry-based* instruction. The spiraling of the PYP around these six themes is one of the most brilliant pieces of the programme flowing from the good works of the original ISCP committees all those years ago.

With all of the above, has this chapter presented *the* answer to its guiding question? By no means! The aim of the chapter is to get the reader thinking, so that when a teacher sits down with his or her colleagues to decide on the 36 units to be addressed in a program of inquiry, the gathered educators will engage even more reflectively in the process. Meanwhile, if we do need to cover fish-grabbing-with-the-bare-hands, we might be able to squeeze this into Physical Education classes!

References

1. Peddiwell, J., and Benjamin, H.R.W. (1939): *Saber-tooth curriculum, including other lectures in the history of paleolithic education*. New York: McGraw-Hill.

2. Boyer, E.: "The Basic School" (speech presented at the National Association of Elementary School Principals' Annual Conference, 1995).

3. Thornburg, D. (2002): *The new basics*. Alexandria, Virginia: Association for Supervision and Curriculum Development (ASCD).

4. Goleman, D. (1995): *Emotional intelligence*. New York: Bantam.

5. Wiggins, G. (1989): The futility of trying to teach everything of importance, in *Educational Leadership*, 47(3), p44.

6. Wiggins, G., and McTighe, J. (1998): *Understanding by design.* Alexandria, Virginia: ASCD.

7. *ibid*, p84.

8. Phenix, P., as cited in Wiggins, G., and McTighe, J. (2005): *Understanding by design.* Alexandria, Virginia: ASCD, p69.

9. Spencer, H., as cited in Broudy, H. (1982): What knowledge is of most worth, in *Educational Leadership*, 39(8), p574.

10. Broudy, H. (1982): What knowledge is of most worth, in *Educational Leadership*, 39(8), p578.

11. Marzano, R. (2003): *What works in schools.* Alexandria, Virginia: ASCD, p26.

12. Ainsworth, L. (2003): *Power standards: Identifying the standards that matter the most.* Englewood, CO: Advanced Learning Press.

13. Blythe, T. (n.d.): *Teaching for Understanding: Throughlines,* retrieved December 15, 2008 from: http://learnweb.harvard.edu/ALPS/tfu/info3b.cfm

14. *ibid.*

15. Eisner, E. (1994): *The educational imagination: On the design and evaluation of school programs.* New York: Macmillan College Publishing Company, 2nd Edition, p87.

16. *ibid*, p93.

17. *ibid*, p97.

18. Boyer, E. (1995): *The basic school: A community for learning.* Hoboken, New Jersey: Jossey-Bass, p81.

19. *ibid.*

20. Carber, S. (2000): Tribal Expressions, in *IB World* 23, pp39-40.

21. Gardner, H., and Perkins, D. (1988): Why zero? A brief introduction to project zero, in *The Journal of Aesthetic Education*, 22(1), pp7-10.

Chapter 4

21st century assessment: what does 'best practice' look like in the PYP?

Ken O'Connor, Rosemary Evans, and Sarah Craig

Introduction

Within the Primary Years Programme framework, the first question asked of educators about assessment is 'How will we know what we have learned?'[1] The question implies the 'we' is both the students and the teachers working together as a community of learners, although the model itself shows the student alone constructing meaning at the centre of the curricular design.[2]

Nonetheless, teachers in a PYP school are encouraged to see themselves as learners, committed to continuous growth over time in their own professional practice. With this in mind, the question intends to guide the thinking of educators about assessment 'best practice' because it asks us how we will know or evaluate what has been learned. In turn, it leads us to think about the types of evidence that will inform our determination of the degree to which a student's acquisition of knowledge, understanding of concepts, and the student's ability to apply skills in a variety of contexts and situations, has developed according to predetermined criteria.

In addition, it prompts teachers to appraise a student's growth with respect to their attitudes about learning, or their 'habits of mind'. Finally, the question asks us to document how students will choose to take action as a result of what they have learned. Each of these areas to be assessed defines a core 'essential element' of the PYP: knowledge; concepts; skills; attitudes and action; and each are germane to what makes the framework unique.

While helpful in providing pedagogical scope, the 'how will we know what we have learned?' question is also somewhat problematic as a prompt for 'best practice' in assessment, because it does not clearly distinguish between the acts of assessment and evaluation. Some leaders in the area of assessment practice do distinguish between the two, and others do not.

However, for the purposes of this chapter, distinguishing between the two is helpful in understanding the difference between assessment for learning and assessment of learning. While assessment is defined as the act of gathering information about student learning that informs our teaching, evaluation involves making a judgement about how much and how well a student has learned. Evaluation is the process of reviewing the evidence we have collected and determining its value.

As teachers, we must make the decision when to assess and when to evaluate, with an eye to the promotion of student learning.[3] Within the PYP, assessment is generally categorized to encompass both assessment and evaluation practice. It includes formative and summative assessment, and the recording and reporting of each.[4] Assessment strategies are defined as observations, performance assessments, process-focused assessments, selected responses and open-ended tasks and tools such as rubrics, exemplars, checklists, anecdotal records and continuums.[5]

Within the realm of reporting, little guidance is defined with respect to grading practices; although a set of communication techniques are recommended including a variety of conferences: student-teacher; teacher-parent(s); student-led; and three-way. Written reports are seen as a summative record of student progress and achievement. However, minimal detail is given about how to report effectively, just that schools must design additional forms of reporting that take into account the PYP and provide clear indication of a student's progress with reference to the IB learner profile. It is notable though, that both the MYP and DP have embedded criterion-based reporting systems based on clearly defined learning expectations and criteria.

Within the assessment framework, the practice of formative assessment or 'assessment *for* learning' now becomes pivotal within a PYP context. When students are acquiring new knowledge, skills, concepts and even attitudes, they need opportunities to practise these without consequences in terms of their grades. While they practise, they need descriptive feedback to help them to make improvements and adjustments as they learn. This is the process of learning, and the primary objective of assessment in a PYP classroom is to provide feedback on the learning process.[6]

At the core of the PYP curricular framework is its emphasis on teaching and learning through concept-driven inquiry. Both the process and products of inquiry are to be assessed independently, and as integrated with one another. Teachers are required to use formative assessment techniques to assess how a student's competency with the inquiry process grows over time.

For instance, do the frequency, depth and complexity of their questions grow over time, are they demonstrating a mastery of the research and thinking skills determined to be essential within the inquiry process, and are they accumulating a comprehensive base of knowledge that helps them to apply their understanding in a variety of contexts?

A set of skills referred to as the 'transdisciplinary skills' are uniquely characterized in a PYP context. The five skill areas comprise a comprehensive, but not exhaustive, list of skills that define and support learning across, among, and between the disciplines. They are the learning skills that are needed for success in the 21st century and are defined within five categories as: research; thinking; communication; self-management and social skills. Collectively, they provided learners with the essential toolkit to exemplify the values and traits laid out in the IB learner profile; that is to be knowledgeable, balanced, caring, principled individuals who are thinkers, communicators and inquirers in an international context and are willing to be open-minded and take learning risks, all while being reflective about themselves and their learning progress.[7]

The planning document used within the PYP, the PYP planner, has been heavily influenced by the work of Grant Wiggins and Jay McTighe in the area of Understanding by Design (UbD). After one significant review cycle, the planner design is even more closely aligned with and premised on the idea that the best curricular planning involves beginning with the end in mind, or starting with the summative assessment first.

When confronted with curricular planning, teachers are asked the question, 'how do we plan for assessment?'[8] At the earliest stages of unit planning, they are prompted to develop summative assessment tasks that are directly linked to the unit's central idea and that allow students to demonstrate their conceptual understanding of this statement. As curriculum designers, teachers are asked to 'think like assessors' rather than 'activity designers' by setting criteria that will clearly distinguish a student's conceptual understanding of the central idea and other related concepts.

All PYP schools are required to adhere to the assessment practices as outlined in the *International Baccalaureate Programme Standards and Practices.*[9] The standards and accompanying practices provide guidelines for schools. While somewhat open-ended, the standards have been written with current 'best practice' in mind, and an eye to possible new practice in the future. The critical standard around assessment, Standard C4, provides the context for a school's approach to assessment and evaluation. It states: 'There is an agreed approach to assessment, and to the recording and reporting of assessment data, which reflects the practices and requirements of the programme.'

The balance of this chapter will attempt to address Standard C4 within the context of the PYP modelling inquiry. We will ask and answer the following questions: What does it look like to have an agreed approach to assessment, and to the recording and reporting of assessment data? What are the specific practices that guide assessment and evaluation practice? Why do we collect diagnostic, formative and summative assessment data? How do these different forms of assessment inform our instructional practice? Which practices provide the best opportunities for students to be active participants in the assessment process? And finally, what is the way forward within our assessment practice in the PYP?

Meeting the standards

Standard C4 provides schools with clear criteria regarding what needs to be put in place to ensure effective assessment, including the requirements for recording and reporting.[10] Standard C4 requires all IB World Schools to develop a school-wide assessment policy. Working collaboratively to develop a school assessment policy provides an opportunity for teachers, administrators, parents and students to attain a common understanding of the place of assessment in the PYP.

The process used to develop and finalize the policy will naturally vary from school to school, but benefits from being broadly consultative. The policy development procedure could involve the following steps:

1. Establish a task force: the task force could include a diversity of perspectives including individuals representing different grade levels, subject areas, including the specialty areas (physical education, the arts, *etc.*), learning support teachers and second language teachers.

2. Review current purposes, principles and practices of assessment including classroom strategies and tools, methods of recording assessment data and reporting mechanisms.

3. Apply Standard C4 to current practice and complete a gap analysis.

4. Conduct a review of best practices in assessment, evaluation and reporting.

5. Draft an assessment policy which meets the requirements of Standard C4, aligns with best practices and the school's mission and vision.

6. Ensure that all agreed upon assessment practices are consistent with the principles and supported by all teachers.

7. Seek feedback on the policy from all stakeholders including parents and all teachers. Some schools develop a simple questionnaire or hold a series of forums.

8. Finalize the policy and share broadly.

9. Review and revise the policy annually based on consultation with all constituents.

The assessment policy should include a statement of principles and policies regarding assessment, which are aligned with Standard C4 and which provide a framework for the school's approach to assessment. Below is a sample statement from one school's policy.

Principles

The primary purpose of assessment and evaluation is to improve student learning. Assessment and evaluation strategies must be varied in nature and allow students to demonstrate the full range of their learning. The assessment of curriculum expectations is separated from the assessment of learning skills and responsibility. Assessment and evaluation practices are fair to all students.

Key areas of focus

1. Assessment involves diagnostic assessment, formative assessment and summative assessment.

2. Learning expectations and criteria for assessment are communicated to students in advance.

3. Students are provided with opportunities to learn how to assess their own work and to set goals for improvement.

4. The use of student portfolios to demonstrate growth over time is encouraged.

5. Students are provided with examples and models to assist them in understanding how to achieve excellence.

6. Peer assessment is used for formative feedback.

7. Teachers provide students with ongoing and descriptive feedback on their learning to assist them to establish goals for improvement.

8. Teachers work collaboratively to determine achievement levels and to establish exemplars.

9. Assessment and evaluation practices accommodate the needs of exceptional students (consistent with their Learning Management Plans) and the needs of students who are learning the language of instruction.

10. Determination of grading levels for formal reporting purposes should primarily reflect student performance on summative tasks. Students' level grades will reflect their most consistent level of achievement with an eye to their most recent levels of achievement at the time of reporting.

11. Informal reporting of student achievement occurs throughout the academic year; formal reporting of student achievement occurs at regular intervals and includes both report cards and parent-teacher interviews. Student involvement in the interview process is encouraged.[11]

As part of an assessment policy, the practices articulated should represent a statement of the essential agreements which all teachers consent to adhere to in their teaching. These practices might address such domains as the practices related to student portfolios and reporting. They might likewise address the school's approach to diagnostic assessment.

Diagnostic assessment: moving beyond KWL

In recent years, changes in literacy and mathematics instructional practice and assessment have also brought changes in the area of diagnostic assessment. Originating with the work of New Zealander Marie Clay, the running record, or miscue analysis, is an individualised performance assessment that teachers use to inform small group and individualised instruction in reading for students.

Conducted at the beginning and then again at key stages in a student's learning process, diagnostic assessments primarily give teachers information about how to better plan and target instruction to meet students' individual needs. Other best practices with a balanced literacy programme, like 'Reader's and Writer's Workshops', also have assessment practices built into their process-based structure.

The teacher assesses student performance regularly and individually through frequent individualised conferences and mini-lessons. Tools such as developmental continua that show how reading, writing and mathematics behaviours and skills are acquired in stages over time can be particularly helpful diagnostic tools in any elementary classroom. Combined with other diagnostic measures like inventories or checklists, teachers are able to gather information about where students are relative to standardised benchmarks or criteria for their age and stage of development. This diagnostic information informs instruction and is often also used to guide the feedback given to students.

In a PYP classroom environment, assessing prior knowledge becomes a key stage in the inquiry process. In order to engage in meaningful structured inquiry with students, it is important for teachers to assess to see what the students already know. In the early years of the PYP, this was predominantly presented to teachers as best achieved using the KWL strategy. That is to ask students to identify what they K: what they already know; W: what they want to learn and then after the inquiry process, L: what they learned.

While this strategy is an effective one, it can become tiresome when used exclusively. Rather, it is important to celebrate prior knowledge but also to challenge students with the types of inquiries that go beyond their knowledge of a topic into a deeper conceptual understanding. A variety of additional techniques are now widely used to support students to document their acquisition of knowledge throughout the inquiry process. What is common to each is that they engage the learner in the same ways as the KWL strategy without using its format and structure.

It is also important to note the significance placed on the teacher questions or provocations for inquiry. These guiding questions provide the frame for the entire unit. They challenge students to conduct research and engage in hands-on activities and experiments to find answers. Teachers are expected to develop units of inquiry organised around a central idea that meet the following criteria. The unit is to be engaging, relevant, challenging and significant.[12] It is often the teacher questions that provide the depth and scope to each of the criteria. In turn, the teacher questions become assessment guides providing formative assessment opportunities for learning throughout the unit leading to the summative assessment at the end.

Assessment for learning: giving feedback along the way

Formative assessment is at the heart of the PYP approach to assessment. As is stated in *A Basis for Practice*, 'The primary objective of assessment in the PYP is to provide feedback on the learning process.'[13] Formative assessment is premised on the belief that every child can improve and become an effective learner when engaged in understanding what good work looks like and when supported to meet learning targets by a range of feedback strategies.

The research support for formative assessment is powerful. Black and Wiliam conducted a review of the literature on formative assessment. Their findings revealed that when teachers use formative assessment effectively the results include improvements in student achievement and student mastery of the skills for lifelong learning.[14] Shirley Clarke has emphasised that what distinguishes formative from summative assessment is the focus on 'deepening and furthering the learning rather than measuring it'.[15] She also emphasises the importance of the child as an active participant in the formative assessment process.

Formative assessment involves:

1. Sharing learning expectations with students.
2. Developing, with students, the criteria for success including criteria for the process and the product or performance.
3. Analysing, with students, real samples of student work.
4. Self and peer assessment.
5. Goal-setting and reflection.
6. Effective feedback.
7. Effective questioning.

All of the above provide opportunities for supporting student growth during the learning process.

Establishing criteria for success

Students need to be involved in developing and clarifying the criteria for success, regarding process, product and performance. Rubrics or checklists which contain words which students do not fully understand are less helpful. Criteria sheets are best constructed using student language.[16] A simple strategy is to have students describe in detail the essential elements of the process, product or performance. They can then classify and categorize their descriptors to produce a criteria checklist with descriptors.[17]

Research skills

Samples of student work, including video tapes and refection sheets and products, can help students to describe what an excellent process or product will look like. The checklists can be 'tested' and revised during the inquiry process.

Anne Davies has identified four pre-requisites for students to fully participate in the assessment and learning process. She explains that students must be supported to understand:

1. Mistakes are essential for learning.
2. The difference between descriptive and evaluative feedback.
3. That they will have the time to try out their ideas.
4. That success has many different looks.[18]

Appreciating the necessity of making mistakes during the learning process is essential to encourage risk-taking. Teachers need to be open with children about their own mistakes and to emphasise that feedback on mistakes is extremely helpful in learning what to do differently.

Formulating questions for a Personal Inquiry

Criteria for Assessment.	Details or Descriptors.
Question is important to the student.	Student indicates a personal interest Student can explain why the question is important to the unit of inquiry.
Question is connected to the central idea.	The question includes key words or concepts which appear in the central idea of the unit of inquiry.
Question can be researched.	There is information about the question available in the school resource centre There are people who the student can interview. There is information on the internet The question provides some direction and focus for the research.
Question involves making a judgment using criteria.	The question requires the student to consider different perspectives. The question requires the student to make a decision or create a new perspective.

Students need to understand that formative feedback is most powerful when it is descriptive as opposed to evaluative. Giving descriptive feedback demands practice on the part of both teachers and students.[19] Descriptive feedback can involve:

1. Telling students to do more of this and less of that.

2. Asking questions: Have you considered?

3. Having students describe how samples of work are similar to the criteria and different from the criteria.

4. Having students use exemplars to identify points for improvement.

Evaluative feedback as part of formative assessment is less effective than descriptive feedback. Black and Wiliam discovered that feedback in the form of descriptions, results in achievement gains while feedback in the form of marks did not, even when combined with verbal feedback.[20]

Students need time to learn effectively and they need to be actively engaged in the learning process. The PYP involves a constructivist approach to learning where students are engaged in such tasks as asking questions, solving-problems, analysing information, making decisions, conducting experiments and investigations, taking responsibility, talking and communicating.

All of these learning tasks take time. As Caren Cameron and her colleagues have noted, we need to 'slow down to the speed of learning' and involve students fully in the process. 'Students need time to:

- set and use criteria;
- self-assess;
- receive and give descriptive feedback;
- collect proof or evidence of learning;
- set and reset their goals;
- seek support for their learning;
- communicate their learning to others.'[21]

Formative assessment can be used in all stages of the structured inquiry process of PYP; indeed it is an essential support for student learning. Formative assessment is also pertinent for assisting students to develop all of the essential elements of the PYP, including knowledge, concepts, skills, attitudes and action.

Assessing growth and understanding in central ideas: supporting concept development

The PYP curriculum is developed to support conceptual understanding. The criteria for demonstrating conceptual understanding include:

1. Correct and precise use of terminology.
2. Correct and appropriate use of examples and non-examples.
3. Appropriate and precise selection of information to illustrate a point.
4. Concise explanations used as required.
5. Few errors in information.
6. Relevant connections made between concepts.[22]

Formative assessment: input for instruction

Formative assessment takes place during the instructional process and provides significant feedback to the teacher to promote adjustments to the teaching plan.

For example, if many students are not able to demonstrate understanding of a key concept or to perform a required skill, additional and varied instruction will be needed. Similarly, formative assessment can help the teacher identify individual students who require scaffolding or support.

Formative assessment of attitudes: a PYP challenge

The formative assessment of attitudes and action requires further discussion. The PYP attitudes are to be addressed 'explicitly within the taught and assessed components of the curriculum so that learning experiences and assessment strategies are designed to support and promote the attitudes'.[23] *Making the PYP Happen* also acknowledges the overlap between the attitudes and the IB learner profile. Student self-assessments and teacher observation are the most powerful strategies for building student understanding and growth toward the PYP attitudes. As Art Costa and Bena Kallick caution, attitudes or habits of mind should not be discussed in terms of mastery, but rather progress and growth.[24]

One strategy which helps students to understand an attitude is to create a T chart which uses student language to describe what one would expect to see, and hear, from a person who is demonstrating the attitude. For example:

Empathy

What does it look like?	What does it sound like?
Mirroring the feelings of others in our facial expressions.	I am trying to understand your point of view...
A hug.	I can see why you are upset...
A supportive smile.	Tell me more about your situation...
	Paraphrasing...

Students can visualise themselves and hear themselves demonstrating the attitudes, and can begin to understand what the attitude is all about and how they can both make progress toward demonstrating the attitude and self-assess their own behaviour.

Formative assessment provides clear and specific feedback to students to help them to meet expectations. It also provides feedback to teachers as they monitor and adjust their teaching strategies. Formative assessment supports both student and teacher learning.

Assessment of learning

Summative assessment occurs at the end of a unit of inquiry, or of a teaching and learning unit for a distinct discipline which falls beyond the programme of inquiry. These assessments are used for the purpose of evaluation or making a judgment and may involve performance tasks, culminating projects, tests or portfolios of work.[25] Summative assessment in the PYP involves students in demonstrating their understanding of the central idea of the inquiry unit as well as all essential elements of the programme.

As we noted earlier, the PYP has been informed by the Understanding by Design (UbD) framework developed by Grant Wiggins and Jay McTighe and this is reflected in the design of the PYP planner. Planning is done with the end in mind. The first page of the planner asks the teacher to consider the summative assessment task and to think about 'possible ways of assessing students' understanding of the central idea'.[26] The teacher is prompted to consider: 'What evidence, including student initiated action, will we look for?'[27] At the beginning of the unit of inquiry the teacher introduces the summative task(s) so that the students are aware of the goal and of the criteria for success in both process and product or performance. As Rick Stiggins suggests, 'Students can reach any target they know about and [which] holds still for them'.[28]

Summative assessment tasks should represent a balance of assessment strategies. There is a place in the assessment repertoire for selected response or short answer assessment methods. Selected response questions require students to select the correct response from a list provided. These methods include: multiple choice, true and false and matching tasks. Short answer questions require students to provide a brief response.

These methods are useful in ascertaining students' knowledge of 'factual information, basic concepts and simple skills'.[29] Although these methods are often seen as 'more objective' forms of assessment, Arter and McTighe caution that the only objective element of these questions is the scoring. Their construction can indeed be very subjective as the teacher has to consider what questions to ask, what wording to use and what incorrect responses to include.[30]

Prior to using these methods to evaluate student knowledge and skills it is always essential to provide students with opportunities to practice these forms of assessment and receive feedback before using them as a basis for evaluative judgment.

Anne Davies contends that, 'demonstrating understanding requires a range of evidence'.[31] Performance tasks provide a rich opportunity for students to show what they know. Performance assessments provide students with authentic applications of their learning. They are frequently used as the culminating assessment tasks for units of inquiry.

Under the transdisciplinary theme 'how we express ourselves' a grade one class engaged in a unit of inquiry focusing on the central idea: 'The way a story is told can make it come to life.' They are given as their culminating task the challenge of turning a well-known simple story into a performance for the junior kindergarten class. The students develop criteria for what makes a good performance to guide their own performances.

Similarly, a grade four class, exploring the transdisciplinary theme 'how we organise ourselves' focuses on the central idea: people create maps to organise and communicate geographic information. Their culminating task includes developing a map, to include landmarks, scale, and cardinal directions, which the class uses to guide their journey to a local science centre.

While not all culminating tasks can be truly authentic, this is a worthy goal. A simple tool to guide teachers in creating authentic performance tasks is the GRASPS Framework. As Tomlinson and McTighe suggest, such tasks readily support differentiation of instruction. The tasks can be customized by 'tweaking' the components to challenge or support individual students. The acronym outlines these components:

1. Select a real world **goal**.
2. Provide a meaningful **role** for the students.
3. Identify an authentic or simulated real world **audience**.
4. Generate a real world problem or **situation** for application of knowledge and skills.
5. Develop with the students **standards** for assessing success.[32]

'Only if we expand and reformulate our view of what counts as human intellect will we be able to devise more appropriate ways of assessing it and more effective ways of educating it'.[33] Within the PYP, it is the culminating task or the 'Exhibition' that provides the richest opportunity for synthesis of the essential elements of the programme.

Recording: sources of evidence

It is important to consider the sources of evidence which will inform teacher judgment regarding student achievement. There are three generally accepted sources of evidence which teachers can use and the use of all three in concert produces the most reliable and valid assessment.

These include: observations of students engaged in learning; products students create; and finally conversations with students about their learning.[34] This three-part approach is called 'triangulation' of evidence and the result is rich assessment information which can ensure our judgments are truly informed.

Grading and reporting

A grade refers to the number or letter reported at the end of a time period which represents a summary of student performance.[35] The primary purpose of giving grades in a PYP school is to provide parents and students with a summary communication about achievement based on agreed learning expectations for the PYP.[36] Grades should be based only on demonstrated student achievement of learning expectations.

Grades should be fair for all students. This does not imply that grades are determined in exactly the same way for all students. Students are not all the same. Their unique differences need to be considered when determining a grade to ensure that fairness is truly present. If a student needs glasses and we deny them the right to wear their glasses because others are not wearing glasses, is this fair? No one would disagree. This applies as well to the student who has a marked learning difference, such as a grapho-motor disability or an attention deficit. To be on an even playing field, students need to be provided with accommodations to ensure that their grades represent a 'fair' assessment of their achievement.[37]

As part of their grading and reporting work, teachers need to develop clear statements of criteria for assessment as well as descriptions of levels of achievement related to each criterion. Students' work samples can be used to assist in the process of distinguishing levels of achievement. These exemplars can help both teachers and students to understand what different levels of achievement related to specific criteria look like.

The following represents a sample from one school's efforts to describe levels of achievement.

3. Nearing proficiency	4. Proficient
The student performs many of the major learning expectations with basic proficiency. Skills are often performed with support. They are generally applied in familiar situations with support.	The student performs many of the major learning expectations at a solid level of proficiency. Skills are performed with little or no support. They are generally applied in familiar situations.
Some understanding.	Considerable understanding.
Generally.	Usually.
Moderately effective/moderate effectiveness.	Effective/effectively.
With moderate assistance/support.	With minimal assistance/support.
Minor inaccuracies that do not affect overall result.	Accurate/accurately.
Moderately/generally clear; able to follow.	Clear/clearly/with clarity; easy to follow.

The determination of grades is an exercise in professional judgment as opposed to an exercise in calculation. Using the mean as a method for determining grades actually penalised students for learning, as results achieved early in the academic year continued to affect a student's grade. Best practice in grading recommends that grades reflect the most consistent achievement of expectations with an eye to the most recent performance. In this way students are not penalised for learning.

Clear meanings of letter grades

Student-led conferencing and portfolios: putting the student at the centre of assessment

A powerful reporting structure often used in PYP schools is the student-led conference. Its effectiveness is enhanced because the practice itself requires students to take on responsibility for reporting what they have learned. Too often, traditional reporting practices, like report cards or parent-teacher conferences, centre on sharing learning achievement from the teacher directly to the parent, omitting the learner themselves.

By requiring the students to conduct the conference, they take on the responsibility to evaluate and reflect upon their work and organise their thoughts about learning well enough to articulate those thoughts to others. Typically, a portfolio of student work becomes the centre piece of the student-led conference. It is the student's selection of the artefacts and his/her reflection on them that provides both the context and the content for the conference. As a learner, the student is empowered to share the process of their learning including their areas of strength and areas in need of strengthening. The portfolio process and the student-led conference combine to provide students with opportunities that make them active participants in sharing and reporting their growth and learning.

Jane Bailey and Thomas Guskey connect the practice of keeping student portfolios with student-led conferencing as the 'process of capturing the "individual voice" is what is exciting and relevant about using portfolio collections to report to parents or others'.[38] The conference provides students with a venue to tell their own learning story. The messages are powerful for students and their parents because of their authenticity and relevance.

Over time, they provide parents with a real 'window' into the intellectual growth and development of their child. Traditional reporting structures only provide parents with information about student learning from the teacher's perspective or through the teacher's 'lens'. While the teacher's perspective is an important one, the child's perspective is essential if parents are to fully understand and appreciate the relevance of their child's learning experiences.[39] Within the student-centred framework of the PYP, keeping student portfolios and conducting student-led conferences become important tools for making students responsible and active participants in their assessment for and of learning.

How will we know what we have learned?

The 'assessment for, of, and as learning', are at the heart of the PYP. When students and teachers are engaged in continuous reflection about the learning process, assessment provides an authentic path for improvement.

References

1. International Baccalaureate Organization, (2007): *Making the PYP happen*. Cardiff: IBO, p44.

2. *ibid*, p7.

3. Davies, A. (2000): *Making classroom assessment work.* British Columbia: Connections Publishing, 1st Edition, p1.

4. International Baccalaureate Organization, (2007): *Making the PYP happen.* Cardiff: IBO, p45.

5. *ibid,* p49.

6. *ibid,* p44.

7. International Baccalaureate Organization, (2005): *IB learner profile booklet.* Cardiff: IBO.

8. International Baccalaureate Organization, (2007): *Making the PYP happen.* Cardiff: IBO, p31.

9. International Baccalaureate Organization, (2005): *International Baccalaureate Programme Standards and Practices.* Cardiff: IBO.

10. *ibid,* p13.

11. Branksome Hall, a three programme IB World School, 2008-2009.

12. International Baccalaureate Organization, (2007): *Making the PYP happen.* Cardiff: IBO, p14.

13. International Baccalaureate Organization, (2009): *A basis for practice.* Cardiff: IBO, p13.

14. Black, P., and Wiliam, D. (2001): *Inside the Black Box,* retrieved on January 13, 2009 from: http://ngfl.northumberland.gov.uk/keystage3ictstrategy/Assessment/blackbox.pdf

15. Clarke, S. (2005): *Formative assessment in action: weaving the elements together.* London: Hodder Murray, p8.

16. Clarke, S. (2003): *Enriching feedback in the primary classroom: Oral and written feedback from teachers and children.* London: Hodder & Stoughton, p7.

17. Davies, A. (2000): *Making classroom assessment work.* British Columbia: Connections Publishing, 1st Edition, p32.

18. *ibid,* p11.

19. *ibid,* p12.

20. Black, P., and Wiliam, D. (2001): *Inside the Black Box,* retrieved on January 13, 2009 from: http://ngfl.northumberland.gov.uk/keystage3ictstrategy/Assessment/blackbox.pdf

21. Cameron, C. *et.al.,* (1997): *Recognition without rewards.* Winnipeg: Portage and Main Press.

22. Arter, J., and McTighe, J. (2001): *Scoring rubrics in the classroom: Using performance criteria for assessing and improving student performance.* Thousand Oaks: Corwin Press, p161.

23. International Baccalaureate Organization, (2007): *Making the PYP happen.* Cardiff: IBO, p25.

24. Costa, A., and Kallick, B., (eds) (2000): *Assessing and reporting on habits of mind.* Alexandria, Virginia: ASCD, pxvii.

25. McTighe, J., and O'Connor, K. (2005): Seven practices for effective learning, in *Educational Leadership,* 63(3), p10.

26. International Baccalaureate Organization, (2007): *Making the PYP happen.* Cardiff: IBO, p13.

27. *ibid.*

28. Stiggins, R. (1997): *Multiple assessment of student progress.* Reston, VA: National Association of Secondary School Principals.

29. Arter, J., and McTighe, J. (2001): *Scoring rubrics in the classroom: using performance criteria for assessing and improving student performance.* Thousand Oaks: Corwin Press, p2.

30. *ibid.*

31. Davies, A. (2000): *Making classroom assessment work.* British Columbia: Connections Publishing, 1st Edition, p26.

32. Tomlinson, C.A., and McTighe, J. (2006): *Integrating differentiated instruction and understanding by design: Connecting content and kids.* Alexandria, Virginia: ASCD, p70.

33. Howard Gardner, as cited in Davies, A. (2000): *Making classroom assessment work.* British Columbia: Connections Publishing, p35.

34. Davies, (2000), p36

35. O'Connor, K. (2007): *A repair kit for grading: 15 fixes for broken grades.* Portland: Educational Testing Service, p7.

36. *ibid*, p8.

37. Branksome Hall, *Level Descriptors for Reporting.*

38. Bailey, J., and Guskey, T. (2001): *Implementing student-led conferences.* Thousand Oaks: Corwin Press, Inc., p2.

39. *ibid.*

Chapter 5

UbD and PYP: complementary planning frameworks

Jay McTighe, Marcella Emberger and Steven Carber

Educators throughout the world work in schools and districts that have adopted the International Baccalaureate Primary Years Programme (PYP)[1] or Understanding by Design (UbD)[2] to promote student inquiry and meaningful learning. Both the PYP and UbD provide frameworks for planning curriculum, assessment and instruction, built around a 'backward design' construct. Indeed, they are complementary, but not identical. This chapter explores the major features of PYP and UbD and highlights key similarities and differences in terms of their goals and approaches to content, assessment and instruction.

The goals of Understanding by Design (UbD)

The goals of UbD are reflected in its title:

1. *Understanding* – A primary goal of education is the development and deepening of student understanding to enable transfer of learning. Evidence of student understanding is revealed when students apply (*ie* transfer) knowledge and skills within authentic contexts.

2. *Design* – Effective curriculum planning reflects a three-stage design process called 'backward design'. By planning with the 'ends' of understanding and transfer in mind, teachers are better able to prioritise their instruction around important ideas while avoiding the problems of 'textbook coverage' and 'activity-oriented' teaching.

The goals of PYP

The PYP is an international, transdisciplinary programme that views structured inquiry as the leading vehicle for learning. The emphasis on transdisciplinary thinking seeks learning across disciplines but with disciplinary lenses. The programme focuses on the total growth of the developing child, seeking to touch hearts as well as minds, encompassing social, physical, emotional and cultural needs in addition to academic welfare.

The PYP intends that students demonstrate the IB learner profile, which includes the descriptors, inquirers, knowledgeable, thinkers, communicators, principled, open-minded, caring, risk-takers, balanced, and reflective. These attributes may at first glance seem to have little to do specifically with internationalism, but the IB[3] suggests that they characterise the types of internationally-minded students that are to be nurtured in IB schools. For a working definition of internationalism, readers are referred to Bartlett and Tangye.[4]

Using UbD in curriculum planning

The UbD framework consists of three stages presented in a design template:

Stage 1: clarifying desired results.

Stage 2: determining acceptable evidence.

Stage 3: developing the learning plan.

Planning with UbD generally begins by considering established goals, such as content standards or learning outcomes. In Stage 1, designers begin by identifying the 'big idea' – those core concepts, principles, theories, and processes contained in established goals that students should come to understand. When planning units, teachers are asked to state the big ideas as enduring understanding; *ie* 'what do we want students to understand and be able to use several years from now, after they may have forgotten the details?' These 'big ideas' are key to understanding the content and making knowledge transferable.

Planners also create or select essential questions based on the targeted understandings. Essential questions serve to 'uncover' the content, provoke thinking, spark connections, and promote the transfer of ideas from one setting to others. Essential questions are inherently open-ended, yielding no single straightforward answer. For example, what makes writing worth reading? (reading and writing); whose 'story' is it? (history and social studies); if practice makes perfect, what makes perfect practice? (music and athletics). Essential questions are typically posted in the classroom and used throughout the unit (or year) to keep the students focused on important ideas.

Next, teachers consider the necessary assessment evidence based on the desired results (Stage 2) and finally the learning plan (Stage 3), including daily lesson plans. It is important to note that while there is a logic to backward design, the actual process is in fact iterative in nature.

The UbD template helps planners check for alignment across the stages, resulting in greater curricular coherence. While originally developed for unit planning, the UbD backward design process has proven equally effective for course (year-long) and programme (multi-year) planning.

Using PYP in curriculum planning

The IB provides a structured unit planner to assist teachers in collaboratively planning for inquiry. The PYP planner is designed around eight open-ended questions, including 'What is our purpose?'; 'What do we want to learn?'; 'How might we know what we have learned?'; 'How best might we learn?'; 'What resources need to be gathered?'; 'To what extent did we achieve our purpose?'; 'To what extent did we include the elements of the PYP?'; and 'What student-initiated inquiries arose from the learning?'[5] The last three sections are completed as a reflection after the inquiry unit concludes, in preparation for the next school year.

Six interdisciplinary themes provide a framework for the exploration of knowledge. These are akin to and inspired by what Boyer[6] called 'core commonalities'. Teachers and students are guided by these themes as they plan and study. According to the *Schools Guide to the Primary Years Programme,* 'students explore subject areas through these themes, often in ways that transcend conventional subject boundaries. In the process, they develop an understanding of important concepts, acquire essential skills and knowledge, develop particular attitudes and learn to take socially acceptable action.'[7]

At the end of a PYP unit, an important question looms large: 'Now that we know this, what will we do?' This is addressed in part by the call to socially responsible student action in section eight of the PYP planner. During the planning process, schools also seek to be attentive to a scope and sequence for each of six subjects – these are school-devised with the use of PYP model documents but they can reflect state or national standards if necessary.

UbD: approach to assessment

In Stage 2, UbD asks educators to 'think like assessors', not activity designers. Teachers consider what types of evidence they will need to determine the degree to which students are developing the knowledge, skills and understandings targeted in Stage 1. Wiggins and McTighe[8] propose that evidence of understanding is revealed through 'authentic' transfer tasks involving one or more of six facets of understanding: explanation; interpretation; application; shifting perspectives; displaying empathy; and exhibiting self-knowledge (reflection and metacognition).

Other evidence of learning is obtained through a variety of assessment methods including quizzes, tests, observations, and work samples. When planning in Stage 2, teachers should consider:

- closely aligning the assessment evidence with the desired results of Stage 1 (validity);
- collecting sufficient evidence of the important goals (reliability);
- establishing an authentic context for performance tasks of understanding/transfer; and
- how feedback will be provided to students.

PYP: approach to assessment

Consideration of assessment begins with the initial 'What is our purpose?' section of the 2007 PYP planner, which corresponds generally with 'Stage 1 – Desired Results' in UbD. Teachers determine a central idea, and are then prompted to complete a sub-section entitled 'Summative Assessment Tasks'. The PYP planner section three, 'How might we know what we learned?' is similar to UbD 'Stage 2 – Assessment Evidence', and prompts teachers to list evidence of learning.

PYP teachers focus on pre-assessment, ongoing assessment, and summative assessment, using a variety of tools for each. Teacher- and student-created rubrics are common and often unique to individual settings. Students place work samples in portfolios as evidence of learning and as material for peer- and self-reflection.

UbD: the teaching and learning plan

In Stage 3 of UbD, teachers develop their plans for teaching and learning based on the desired results of Stage 1 and the assessments in Stage 2. Guided by the acronym WHERETO, designers consider a set of questions that help them plan the unit's lessons:

W = What prior knowledge and understanding (or misconceptions) do students have about the content?

H = How will students know the goals and expected performances of the unit? How will we hook and hold students' interests?

E = How will we help students develop the targeted understandings and equip for their transfer performances?

R = How will we help students rethink or revise their understandings?

E = How will students self-evaluate and reflect on their learning?

T = How will the learning be tailored for diverse students in the classroom?

O = How will the learning be best organised and sequenced?

As designers answer these questions, they keep focused on the 'end' – what we want students to understand and be able to apply (transfer).

PYP: the teaching and learning plan

Teachers often 'frontload' a PYP unit by teaching requisite knowledge and skills and then they transfer partial responsibility of instructional planning to the students. This frontloading phase enables teachers to address established content standards, while the second phase honours the PYP's emphasis on student inquiry. According to Short, '…inquiry-based instruction involves students "asking their own questions". They immerse themselves in a topic and have time to explore in order to find questions that matter to them – they don't just research someone else's topic or question.'[9]

Exemplary PYP classrooms feature a variety of individual projects in response to students' own original queries, in formats such as posters, PowerPoints, skits, original videos, and purposeful essays. Because of the many diverse settings around the world in which the PYP is practiced, students will encounter a wide repertoire, a 'mixed salad', of techniques drawn from numerous international teachers.

Comparing curriculum planning with UbD and PYP

Both UbD and PYP follow a 'backward design' approach to curriculum design and both provide templates to guide the planning process. Each encourages a collaborative approach to planning, whereby teachers work with a partner or a team to design units. However, the frameworks differ somewhat on their approach to curriculum 'content'.

PYP calls for a transdisciplinary approach to curriculum through the use of established themes, whereas UbD units typically develop around established standards within disciplines. Teachers using the PYP planner build the unit around a single central idea and related questions, while UbD units typically feature several enduring understandings and concomitant essential questions.

It is important to note that the PYP planner was developed for use at the primary school level (grades K-5) where cross-curricular teaching flourishes. UbD offers a more universal framework that is being used to plan curriculum from pre-K to university levels. At the secondary and collegiate levels, curriculum is more often framed around specific disciplines. Consequently, UbD units at these levels are more likely to be content specific. Of course, UbD can be used to plan interdisciplinary curriculum as long as the 'big ideas' and essential questions of the connected content areas are properly honoured.

In terms of assessment, both PYP and UbD call for a collection of evidence – a 'photo album' rather than a single 'snapshot'. UbD explicitly asks for evidence of understanding, collected via the six facets along with 'other evidence' of knowledge and skill acquisition. Both frameworks recommend establishing an 'authentic' context for assessment tasks, and UbD uses the acronym GRASPS as a tool for creating such tasks. PYP places a premium on collecting student work in portfolios. Both frameworks employ criterion-based evaluation using rubrics, and encourage students to self-assess and reflect against established performance standards.

Instructionally, both frameworks emphasise active learning whereby students are engaged in 'constructing meaning'. Both PYP and UbD utilise teacher-created essential/guiding questions. However, PYP is more overt about encouraging students to generate their own inquiry questions. UbD embraces the principles and practices of differentiated instruction,[10] while PYP stresses personalised learning through the student-generated inquiries. The PYP includes a valuable 'call to action' at the conclusion of units to encourage both teachers and students to consider questions such as: *so what? What's next? How can we use what we have learned?*

UbD provides a robust set of 'design tools' and examples to support curriculum planning. Because of the complementary nature of the two frameworks, teachers in PYP schools have found many of the UbD design tools to be very congruent with the planner.

UbD users are able to 'work smarter' through the www.ubdexchange.org website, an online system for collaborative designing and reviewing units of study. Thousands of UbD units are available via its searchable database so that teachers do not need to reinvent the wheel when planning commonly taught topics.

Similarly, PYP practitioners utilise the Online Curriculum Center (OCC) at: www.occ.ibo.org/ibis/occ/guest/home.cfm Users can access a sample programme of inquiry as well as scope and sequence documents. Additionally, the OCC offers culminating project (PYP exhibition) guidelines and links to research flowing from the IB Research Unit located at the University of Bath in the United Kingdom.

Both UbD and PYP stress the value of regular reviews of curriculum and assessment designs, which in the case of UbD are based on the UbD Design Standards and a Peer Review process. Both frameworks recommend that textbooks be used as resources rather than as a syllabus.

In conclusion: a call to collaboration

Although originating independently, Understanding by Design and the Primary Years Programme share many philosophical and practical elements. As evidenced by recent PYP-related conference presentations around the globe, the PYP is now taking a more active role in articulating its practice in UbD terms. Indeed, the stage is set for practitioners from both approaches to 'cross-pollinate' their classroom practices by learning from each other. It is the hope of the authors that this chapter will serve to herald expanded communication and collaboration among users of the two frameworks.

Questions to contemplate

- How are UbD and PYP similar in their goals of engaging students and developing understanding? What are some differences?

- What elements of either framework can strengthen the other? (For example, the PYP notion of understanding could be clarified with the six facets of understanding, while the idea of more personalised student inquiries may be of interest to UbD educators.)

- What are the advantages of framing 'the content' of teaching and assessing around established content standards *vs* allowing students' interests to be more directive? What place do locally mandated content standards have in public PYP schools? Do they need a place?

- What is the role of teacher-developed essential questions (with some 'end' in mind)? What is the role of student-generated questions?

- To what extent do the PYP planner and the UbD template support teacher thinking or restrict teacher creativity?

- How are assessments designed and used within both programmes to support student learning?

- In designing a unit, how does a writer decide 'how many' enduring understandings to create? Is a single central idea sufficient?

- How important is it for students to create their own questions and explore their own answers? If UbD planners create essential questions from the big ideas, is that sufficient, or should students be allowed to go in pursuit of their own questions and answers?

- To what extent can (and should) the PYP emphasis on transdisciplinary curriculum and student-generated inquiries be applied to the curriculum for older students (beyond the primary years)?

- In UbD, content standards are considered to hold the big ideas of each discipline. What is 'falling through the cracks' if curriculum planning stays within traditional disciplines?

- How might teachers in both programs 'work smarter' and share their best ideas?

This chapter is a reprint of an article that appeared in the November 2008 issue of the International Schools Journal, Vol xxviii, No 1, p25, *published by John Catt Educational Ltd. It has been modified for this book format and is reprinted with permission.*

References

1. International Baccalaureate Organization. (2007): *Making the PYP happen.* Cardiff: IBO.

2. Wiggins, G., and McTighe, J. (1998): *Understanding by design.* Alexandria, Virginia: ASCD.

3. International Baccalaureate Organization, (2003): *A schools' guide to the primary years programme.* Cardiff: IBO.

4. Bartlett, K., and Tangye, R. (2007): *Defining internationalism in education through standards,* retrieved January 14, 2009 from: http://intranet1.canacad.ac.jp:3445/strategic/admin/download.html?attachid=301578

5. International Baccalaureate Organization, (2007): *PYP Planner.* Cardiff: IBO, pp1-4.

6. Boyer, E. (1995): *The basic school: a community for learning.* Hoboken, New Jersey: Jossey-Bass, p81.

7. International Baccalaureate Organization, (2003): *A schools' guide to the primary years programme.* Cardiff: IBO, p6.

8. Wiggins, G., and McTighe, J. (1998): *Understanding by design.* Alexandria, Virginia: ASCD.

9. Short, K. (1997): Inquiring into inquiry, in *Learning*, 25, p55.

10. Tomlinson, C.A., and McTighe, J. (2006): *Integrating differentiated instruction and understanding by design: Connecting content and kids.* Alexandria, Virginia: ASCD, p70.

Chapter 6

English as a Second Language

Brian Dare

Introduction

Over the last decade, international schools have experienced ever-increasing enrolments of English as a Second Language (ESL) students. With this has come a particular set of challenges which schools need to address if these students are to enjoy the same educational outcomes as non-ESL students. There are a range of effective responses that international schools can make to this challenge that include valuing and supporting ESL students' first language, employing ESL specialists to work in intensive English and mainstream classrooms and providing professional development opportunities for teachers in ESL pedagogy as part of a whole school approach.[1]

A key component of any long term whole-school focus on supporting ESL students is the teaching and learning practices that go on in each and every classroom in the school. Most ESL students will spend most of their time in mainstream classrooms, emphasising the responsibility all teachers have in ensuring that their ESL students have equal access to the curriculum. This chapter should be seen as a starting point to helping mainstream teachers build a rich and supportive pedagogy that will see all ESL students reaching their potential. It will also point to resources and professional development programs that will build on the understandings described here.

Much of what follows is based on the importance of language in teaching and learning. ESL students have both to learn in English while learning English, which means they invariably have some catching up to do if they are to build up their English language resources for making meaning across an increasing range of contexts. As those who have long been working in the field have argued, the most effective way of building up these resources is through an explicit pedagogy in which teachers and students are co-constructors of meaning in a supportive environment.[2]

I will begin by looking briefly at what could be grouped under 'affective' issues: those things that impact on making the students feel like they belong in your classroom. If ESL students feel happy, safe and welcomed in your classroom, you have laid a vital foundation for successful learning. The major focus of the article, though, will be on the pedagogy itself. I will outline how we can use oral interactions, both teacher to student and student to student, as a rich resource for speeding up students' language development. This will also provide a very appropriate bridge into looking at ways of supporting ESL students with their writing through a rich teaching learning cycle.

Building positive affective states

As for all students, the first step in supporting ESL students is to make sure that your classroom is a place where they will be willing and able to learn. However, for ESL students this is often far more challenging because of the varying levels of English they bring to the classroom. They will feel under considerable pressure as they try to draw on limited English resources to express their immediate needs as well as the more complex meanings demanded of them by the curriculum. For many ESL students this is a very new experience as they suddenly find themselves struggling in these new contexts which demand that they draw on a very different set of linguistic and cultural resources.

The set of resources that an ESL student bring may differ markedly from those that you draw on in your classroom. Sometimes this is very obvious, for example when you have a student coming with both a language that is very different in its script and in its grammar from English, and from an educational system that values a very different set of pedagogical practices to those operating in your international school. In building ESL students access to both English and these 'new' pedagogical practices we need to be mindful that we don't make students feel like they have something 'missing'.

A very important starting point in setting up a positive and effective learning environment is recognising and valuing what ESL students bring from other contexts. One highly effective way to do this is to show that you value a student's home language and do not see it as some kind of hindrance to their learning. This can be as simple as learning to pronounce a student's name as correctly as possible or learning a few simple greetings and phrases of praise in their language. It can also mean showing sensitivity to how you encourage students to use their home language inside and outside the classroom.

Many are tempted to ban students from using their first language at school. This is counter-productive because our language is our major meaning-making system and, at least initially, students will be drawing heavily on their home language and attempting to translate these meanings to and from English. Educators such as Gallagher[3] and Carder[4] have long argued against such practices, pointing out the negative impact on both their mother tongue and English language development.

Our language is so inextricably bound up with our sense of identity that making such rules will be read as highly offensive. Banning the first language also means we don't have the opportunity to draw on the rich linguistic resources that students bring.[5] One of the most significant ways we can value their home language is through formal mother tongue maintenance programs in the school. Many international schools have been very pro-active in this regard, setting up programs that reflect the linguistic composition of their student cohort.

There are many other ways we can value what students bring to the classroom. This can be as simple as spending some time with a student, particularly if they are new to the school, to find out in a non-intrusive way about their lives: what they like doing in their spare time; what they read; something of their cultural and linguistic backgrounds and so on. We can make a point of including and valuing their life experiences as part of the learning going on in the classroom, but without making them the focus as some kind of 'exotic other'.

You can also be aware that they are forging new and shifting identities in this new environment and let them know that you understand the kinds of tensions this might bring.[6] Another strategy is to acknowledge previous learning by making sure that whenever new work on a particular topic is undertaken, you make a point of finding out what that student already knows about that topic in their first language. We can also reflect the experiences, beliefs and cultural groupings of all our students through the selection of the materials we use in the classroom.

Shifting to learning English and learning in English

However, we cannot allow ourselves the luxury of just making the students feel good about themselves. They need access to the ways of meaning embedded in any given curriculum. ESL students have the same rights to success as any other student, but unless they get the right kind of support they will not reach their potential. The figure below, adapted from Mariani,[7] will be helpful here in framing the kind of pedagogical practices which I see as most productive for all students but particularly so for ESL students.

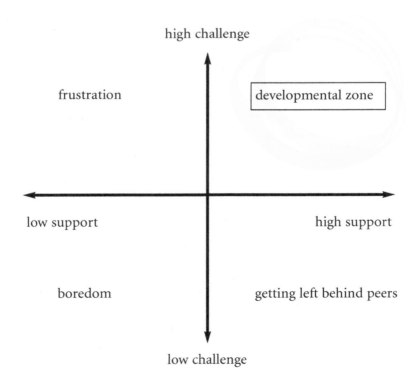

Here we see two axes: the horizontal axis which is concerned with the level of support we give students, moving from low to high and the vertical with the degree of challenge students face when attending to meaning as they read, write, listen and speak. It is instructive at this point to imagine yourself in the role of an ESL learner and think about how you would feel if you found yourself experiencing the kind of pedagogy that characterises each quadrant.

So how would you react to being in a learning situation with high challenge and low support? Frustrated? Angry? Disillusioned? Struggling? And what about a context with low support with low challenge? Boredom? Frustration again? Moving to the high support/low challenge quadrant will possibly increase the comfort levels for many students but there is a very good chance they will be left in the wake of their peers if they spend most of their time here. The ideal quadrant is the high challenge/high support quadrant. Here, in this developmental zone, if we can provide the right kind of scaffolding with just the right kind of challenge, we will see our students making good progress.

A key feature of this developmental zone is that there is a strong interventionist role for the teacher.[8] I will suggest two broad areas we can look at here: first, *the kinds of interactions* we set up between us, as the teacher, and the students as well as those between students themselves. Secondly, I will focus on a *teaching learning cycle* that arose out of work in contexts with very high proportions of ESL students.[9] The key focus of this teaching learning cycle is that we move through four broad stages in any given unit of work, with each stage providing particular opportunities to develop and support ESL students through what we will see is macro-scaffolding and micro-scaffolding. In this way, ESL students will be initially supported through strong scaffolding in the early stages of the curriculum cycle, so that they can operate more independently at a later point in the cycle where they will have more resources to complete the major task of the unit.

Teacher-student spoken interactions

Many working in the child language development field over the last 30 years have argued that, far from being a 'natural, internal process', a child's language development hinges crucially on the interactions between the child and the adults who figure prominently in that child's life.[10] Others[11] have also argued that it is through social interaction that children learn and that the 'expert' adult plays a critical role in setting up the kinds of interactions that will allow this learning to take place.

If we take this view, then the nature of the interactions we provide for our students to engage in will be a critical determinant of how much and how quickly their language resources build. With this in mind, we will now focus on how we can make the everyday interactions that go on in the classroom a productive resource for not only accelerating the uptake of English, but also a rich foundation for moving students from their common sense everyday understandings of the world to the more complex, technical and formal meanings they are expected to make in schooling.

If an ESL student is to develop their English, then they will need as many opportunities to use the language in as many meaningful contexts as possibly can be provided. Teachers are a prime resource for the ESL students here, but if all we do is provide a 'sea of blah',[12] then the students are going to either switch off because they don't understand the meanings or they will be bored or frustrated, or a bit of both. ESL students are more likely to switch off because of their limited English resources. They need to be much more fully engaged in the process and there are ways to go about our teaching which will ensure that this happens.

A good starting point for making any interaction meaningful is to think about having language accompanying action rather than language itself being the focus. An ideal starting point for ESL students is to provide contexts where they can take up the meaning of the words and wordings you use because they are context embedded. If I hold up a test tube in science and say "This is a test tube" and then a pipette and say "And this is a pipette" then it is highly likely that all the ESL students will understand.

If I stop and write or display the words 'test tube' and 'pipette' as well, this will reinforce the word visually, thus helping with pronunciation and reading. If I say the following "Here is the test tube. Using the pipette, I am going to add two drops of acid to the test tube" while demonstrating these actions, then ESL students will understand. As we move away from more concrete objects to abstract concepts we can still use this principle even when referring to more abstract images.

Imagine that, as you say "the thin blue line going from the vertex to the point A" or the "smaller of the two circles", you are actually running your finger along the blue line or around the smaller of the two circles. Referring to diagrams of any kind in this way will make it more meaningful to the students. This may seem trite, and it will be if only done every now and then, but where it is a consistent and systematic part of your teaching practice it will become a powerful tool that will allow your students to understand your meanings even with more abstract topics.

We can use this principle of language accompanying action and apply it to other activities where the students take on a more active role. For example, imagine you are an art teacher and you want your students to be able to take a good black-and-white photo portrait. You could demonstrate how to do this with the students watching.

You could explain the procedure as you go along (being mindful of the principle of language accompanying action of course!) and then hand out the written procedure for your students to follow the steps as they then work in groups to produce their own photo. But a simple reversal of roles here might be far more effective. Using the principle of language accompanying action, we could hand out the procedure first and ask the students in turns to 'command' you (and you could play the 'uncomprehending idiot' so that they are very clear with their instructions).

You can take the opportunity to repeat the command or, as the case may be, even paraphrase where you think necessary, so that they are using the language and you are doing the actions, demonstrating the action itself. This allows the students to both take a more active role but also have the opportunity to use language in a meaningful context.

As we engage in the various activities of the classroom as described above, there are many other ways we can support our ESL students through the conscious use of particular language strategies. One of the most obvious ways teachers engage their students in learning is through asking questions. However, as we will see, some of the common patterns of questioning we engage in typical classrooms can be limiting.

Consider the following dialogues between teachers and students:

Transcript 1

Teacher   Have you got any toy animals? S- (Name of child) [Initiation]

Student   (Standing up) I have got a cat, a [Response]

Teacher   No, sit down, in your place. [Feedback]

From Candlin and Mercer (2001)[13]

Transcript 2

Teacher   What do I mean by opposite operations? [Initiation]

Student   It's opposite [Response]

Teacher   Yeah. [Feedback] So if I have plus what do I do? [Initiation]

Students   Minus [Response]

Teacher   Okay, that's what I mean by opposite operations [Feedback][14]

What we see here is what has been identified by researchers[15] as the IRF pattern: I for initiation, R for response and F for feedback. As Mercer points out[16] not only is this a very common pattern across English speaking schools but 'research shows that this particular kind of use of question-and-answer by a teacher – asking questions to which the teacher knows exactly what answers (s)he seeks – is the most common function of IRFs in classrooms. Here students are essentially trying to provide the information that the teacher expects them to know.'(p245).

While these interactions are sometimes appropriate and very useful, it is very limiting if it is the only way we use questions. If it is the only strategy we have then we are putting a lot of pressure on the students, particularly ESL students, because we are constantly putting them in the role of 'knower'. Moreover, because they most often involve short responses we are not pushing the students into using extended text, something that will be even more critical for their writing.

There are a number of strategies we can adopt to avoid relying on the IRF pattern. We will use the following transcript of a highly skilled ESL teacher (T) working with very young children,[17] one of whom is using a story map to re-tell the story that they have read in class. As we will see, she uses a number of different strategies to support her student, My (M), to build up her English language resources.

Transcript 3

1. T   My, this is an interesting story map. Tell us what's happening here.

2. M   The giant said, "Get me some bread or I hit you with my bommy knocker". And the, the people get some bread some the, um, um, the giant...

3. T   Yes, they gave the bread to the giant.

4. M   "Get me some butter. Get me some butter or I hit you with my bommy knocker". And the people get some, some, um, get some butter and give to the giant.

5. T   Yes, they gave the butter to the giant.

6. M   Yeah, and the giant said, "Get me some, some honey or I hit you with my bommy knocker". And the people find everywhere in honey, can't see it.

7. T   They looked everywhere, didn't they?

8. M   Yeah, yeah, and look in the bridge and looking in...

9. T   Whereabouts in the bridge did they look?

10. M   Oh (draws people on map).

11. T   Uh, huh. Where are they?

12. M   Under.

13. T   They looked under the bridge, did they? OK, and did they look on top of the bridge, too?

14. M   Yes.

15. T   Uh, huh. Keep going...

We can see a number of very supportive strategies being undertaken here. The first thing to notice from the opening utterance from the teacher is that this whole activity is built around language accompanying action. "This is an interesting story map" shows that they are both looking at My's story map as a support for her re-telling. In line 1, we see the teacher handing over responsibility to My to start the re-telling because she has some confidence that My will be able to do so. In line 3, we see the teacher recasting My's last sentence and in doing so provides not only the missing words but also the grammatical structure for her.

Notice how My takes this up in line 4 but still makes a mistake with the tense. Immediately, the teacher recasts her wordings (line 5) again providing the appropriate language. We see this interaction repeated in lines 6-8 as My takes up the teacher's wordings and uses the word 'look' twice in one utterance. Also see the way the teacher uses tag questions (didn't they, haven't you, is she...) to confirm the meaning and prompt use of a particular grammatical structure.

We can also see the teacher using 'Wh' questions effectively to get My to use the preposition 'under' which she does in line 12. With this kind of negotiation of meaning happening, it is no surprise that My was able to eventually produce an effective independent re-telling of the story.

As noted earlier, we often see students not given the opportunity to produce extended stretches of text and, in fact, the use of questioning that produces the IRF pattern can contribute to this. When Gibbons discusses this in her chapter on classroom talk,[18] we see her arguing that we should be 'stretching' and 'pushing' students' language. Consider the following dialogue:

Transcript 4

Teacher	What did you have to measure?
Student	The distance.
Teacher	Which distance?
Student	The distance from the vertex.
Teacher	Which vertex?
Student	(pointing) That one.
Teacher	Can you be more precise?
Student	The outside of the other shape?
Teacher	I'm not sure where you mean, where on the shape?
Student	The bottom left hand corner.
Teacher	OK and what do we call that shape?
Student	The object.
Teacher	OK. So the line's going to...
Student	The bottom left vertex of the object.
Teacher	OK. Who can put all that together and tell me what you're measuring. What distance?
Student	The distance from the top left hand vertex of the image to the bottom left vertex of the object.

Here we see a teacher using a series of questions that push the students to extend their thinking with each exchange and even teases the students by taking on the role of someone who doesn't understand because the instructions are not precise enough. Importantly, note what happens at the end. She asks the question "Now who can put all that together?" which gives the student a chance "to use stretches of discourse in contexts where there is press on their linguistic resources".[19] Here we see the teacher deliberately pressing the students into the extended stretch of text "The distance from the top left hand vertex of the image to the bottom left vertex of the object."

Another very useful strategy, particularly with reading a difficult text with the students, is through the use of what has been termed preformulation.[20] The idea here is that before asking the students questions you provide enough prior knowledge to your students so that they will almost certainly be able to answer the questions that follow. By building up enough shared understandings, you will ensure that your students can much more successfully respond to your questions. It ensures that the students are not playing the 'guess what is in my head' game but more importantly makes clear what the 'new' learning is. Consider a situation where you are reading the following text as a whole class activity:

> The life cycle of the ant consists of four stages: egg, larva, pupa, and adult.
>
> In the first stage, the queen ant mates with one or more male ants and then seeks a nest to lay the eggs to form an ant colony. Ant eggs are tiny: they are approximately 0.5mm in diameter and weigh about 0.0005g. They are oval shaped and have a smooth sticky surface, which enables them to bond together in a mass and be moved about quickly by adult ants.

A possible preformulation for this text might look something like: "Okay, the following text is about the life cycle of an ant, which actually goes through a number of stages. Four main stages. And they are listed in the first paragraph." You could then ask the students to read the first paragraph and ask them to see if they can identify the four stages listed. With this preformulation in place we can expect that the students will be able to answer questions such as: "How many stages are there in the ant life cycle?" or "What is the first stage? And the second stage?" and so on.[21]

For the second paragraph, the preformulation might go something like: "Now the second paragraph is all about the first stage, the egg stage." The question that follows might then be: "What wordings in the first sentence tell us that this paragraph is about the first stage?" We could then ask the students to underline the wordings 'in the first stage'. We could then follow this up with: "How do we know it is about the egg stage?" Once the students respond, you can take up the opportunity to either reformulate or elaborate on what the student says to develop the students' understanding and knowledge.[22]

For some, this may seem like spoon-feeding but what it does is make sure that all the students, including the ESL students, will understand exactly what the text is about. And of course you can vary the degree and intensity of preformulation reformulation as the context demands. As your students take up the meanings you are expecting of them they will inevitably move to independence as they work through any given topic. These kinds of pre- and re-formulations become even more critical as the complexity of the texts students are expected to read increases.

Student-student interactions

In the interactions described above we have focused primarily on the teacher and looked at the different ways we can support our ESL students through deliberate and purposeful interventions. Another resource we can use is the students themselves. As we have stated, ESL students will develop their language through using the language, and one way we can enrich the interactions in the classroom (and avoid that 'sea of blah' again) is to provide opportunities through group work for rich and productive interactions between students.

At its best, this can provide opportunities for ESL students to interact with their more English-proficient peer students to use language in a purposeful and non-threatening environment. Gibbons[23] argues that group work offers 'considerable message redundancy – that is, similar ideas will be expressed in a variety of different ways. Asking questions, exchanging information and solving problems all provide a context where words are repeated, ideas are rephrased, problems are restated and meanings are refined.'[24]

However, just putting students in groups and expecting all the above benefits to materialise is fraught with danger. Any group work must be carefully and intentionally organised.[25] We can't assume students know how to do group work, so they will need support and practice. In addition, with our ESL students, we must always keep in mind the kinds of linguistic resources they will need to function effectively as part of the group. So when organising roles within any given group we need to focus on what language will be needed to carry out that role.

We can see that taking on the role of timekeeper in a group will not be as linguistically difficult as taking on the role of reporting back to the whole class. This does not mean we do not 'press' our ESL students into the role of reporting back, but ensure that we very consciously think about how we can prepare the ESL students for that role. This would apply to any activity in which ESL students are involved.

Take an example where you set up a jigsaw activity[26] in which each group was expected to read a text, make notes and then report those findings to a newly-formed group. You could support less proficient ESL students by pairing them up with more proficient peers; or you could do some earlier preparatory work (think of preformulation principle) with the group of ESL students, who you think might struggle with this jigsaw task, so that they will have sufficient resources to at least participate effectively in the activity.

Moving from speaking to writing

Up until now, we have focused mainly on spoken interactions, both those between teachers and students and between the students themselves. We now shift to how we can support ESL students with their writing, through consideration of an explicit teaching learning cycle[27] which has been taken up enthusiastically by many educators working in contexts with large numbers of ESL students.[28]

The teaching learning cycle outlined in the diagram overleaf provides a broad framework for organising a carefully scaffolded series of learning activities which will provide the macro-scaffolding for the kinds of micro-scaffolding strategies outlined above. In this way we will prepare students for reading and writing the texts demanded of them as they move through any given unit of work. While a particular genre (an information report, a recount, a narrative, an argument and so on[29]) provides the basis for the explicit teaching of key textual and linguistic features of that genre, this is done as part of a myriad of other rich and interesting activities that will allow students to develop the curriculum knowledge of the particular topic.

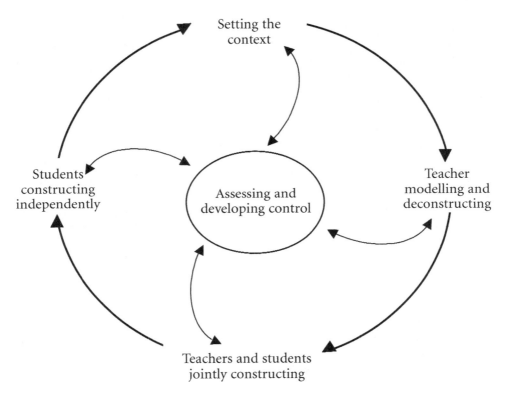

Setting the context

Students constructing independently

Assessing and developing control

Teacher modelling and deconstructing

Teachers and students jointly constructing

Developing a range of genres and registers

From the Teaching ESL Students in Mainstream Classroom Teacher Development Course

In setting the context for learning stage, we engage the students in a number of activities which will, from the outset, raise their interest in the particular topic under focus, establishing at the same time what students already know about aspects of that topic. From here, we can begin to build on and develop these understandings through various activities such as going on excursions, viewing videos, exploring relevant internet sites, inviting in guest speakers and setting up class and small group discussions.

We can see how these activities can provide plentiful opportunities for students to talk their way into understanding the topic, providing, as they do, recycling of the kind of language the students will need when they move to the independent construction stage (remember 'message redundancy'!). Importantly, they also provide us as teachers with rich opportunities to use the interactions discussed earlier, for building all students' language resources as they go about building up shared knowledge of the topic. At this early stage of the cycle, we would also make it clear which genre will be under scrutiny throughout the unit, as students will be expected to produce their own example in the independent stage.

The next stage, the deconstructing and modeling stage, sees teacher and students closely examining examples of the genre that the students will be expected to produce at a later stage. For example, we might be focusing on sequential explanations (such as the life cycle of the ant seen earlier) or on an information report on dolphins or on procedural text on how to do something. These texts will differ in their purpose and they will have different schematic structures.

If the students have never met such texts before then we would need to familiarise them with the purpose of such texts and explore the various phases the texts go through to achieve their purpose. An argument, for instance, typically outlines (in the opening paragraph known as the thesis) the various reasons you agree or disagree with a particular proposal and then subsequent paragraphs take up each argument with supporting details. It finishes with a concluding paragraph which brings the argument together and restates the thesis, often adding some recommended course of action.

This stage also gives us the chance to look at key language features associated with any given genre. To use a very obvious example, consider the following procedure:

PATTY CAKES

Ingredients

3 tablespoons of butter; 1 cup self-raising flour; ¼ cup caster sugar; pinch salt; 1 egg; ¼ cup milk; ¼ teaspoon vanilla.

Method

1. Beat butter and sugar to a cream.
2. Add lightly beaten egg and vanilla. Beat well.
3. Sift flour and salt together.
4. Fold in dry ingredients alternately with milk and mix well.
5. Drop heaped teaspoonfuls of mixture into well greased patty tins.
6. Bake in a moderately hot oven for ten to 15 minutes.
7. Cool on a wire rack.
8. Ice with butter icing.

In terms of its schematic structure it follows a very typical pattern (title [goal] then list of ingredients then method). We could usefully explore with students how we recognise those stages through such things as different headings with different size fonts, some bolded, one in large caps. We can also discuss what is happening in the language as well. An excellent place to start exploring the grammar with students is to get them to focus on how the sentences are beginning in the method section.

If we ask them what action are we expected to do in the first step we could circle the word 'Beat'. Repeating this for the rest of the sentences would reveal a pattern here: that action verbs seem to appear at the front of the sentence in procedures. This of course is not a pattern we see in other sentences in English; nor is necessarily a pattern we would see in other languages. At this point, you could ask if any of your ESL students are able to translate some of the above sentences into their home language and by asking the same questions as above you could identify where (if at all) the action verbs are located, focusing on how the two languages are similar and how they differ. This process can be instructive for the other students in the class to see that other languages do it differently. It is also just another small way you can value the home languages that ESL students bring to the classroom.

The third broad stage has teachers and students jointly constructing the kind of text that they will soon have to write independently. It is very important that the students have built up considerable knowledge both of the genre itself and the topic of the unit by the time they reach this stage. As you and the students go about co-constructing the text, you invite contributions from the students. They will have developed considerable expertise in the topic under study and with their new knowledge of both the topic and the genre they will be very keen to contribute to this co-construction.

However, you as the more expert writer will draw on your expertise to accept or reframe the various contributions. Some you will have to reject or judiciously put to one side, but once students get used to this it will not bother them in the least. They will see the text as a joint effort and not a reflection of their own abilities. You can see how useful the interaction we discussed earlier on comes into play here as you recast, reshape and elaborate on the contributions of the students to produce a text that will be much better written than they could have produced on their own.

In the final stage, students will be expected to move towards an independent construction. How independent the students are will depend on how familiar they are with the genre and with the topic they will be writing about. If they are very new to a genre you might begin a new cycle and build interest in another topic, with students maybe choosing their own related topic (a different animal for instance if you were focusing on information reports). We also need to add that we can move in and out of the cycle into mini-cycles, as we see the need to go back over something, or work on some area that we hadn't foreseen, when planning the unit.

Conclusion

It was stated earlier that the best teaching context to speed up the learning of ESL students is one which provides high support along with high challenge. In arguing for high challenge we are saying that ESL students have every right to access the same curriculum as other students. However, the degree of access is largely determined by the extent of their English language resources.

So the high challenge must be coupled with high support in quickly building those resources. Outlined above are a number of micro- and macro-scaffolding techniques that, when applied systematically and judiciously, will be a significant step in doing exactly that. Experience in working with teachers, who have ESL students in their classrooms, from contexts all over the world, has shown that adopting an explicit pedagogy around language provides a rich learning environment not only for ESL students but all students.

References

1. Gallagher, E. (2008): *Equal rights to the curriculum: Many languages, one message.* Clevedon: Multilingual Matters; (and) Dare, B., Custance, B., and Polias, J. (2006): *Teaching ESL students in mainstream classrooms: Language and learning across the curriculum.* Hindmarsh SA, Australia: DECS Publishing.

2. Schleppegrell, M. (2004): *The language of schooling: A functional perspective.* New Jersey: Lawrence Erlbaum Associates; (and) Gibbons, P. (2002): *Scaffolding language, scaffolding learning: Teaching second language learners in the mainstream classroom.* Portsmouth, NH: Heinemann; (and) Rose, D. (2005): Democratising the classroom: a literacy pedagogy for the new generation, in *Journal of Education,* 37, 2005; (and) Polias, J., and Dare, B. (2004): Towards a pedagogical grammar, in *New Directions in Language and Education,* McCabe, A., O'Donnell, M., and Whittaker, R. (eds). London: Continuum.

3. Gallagher, E. (2008): *Equal rights to the curriculum: Many languages, one message.* Clevedon: Multilingual Matters.

4 Carder, M. W. (2007): *Bilingualism in International Schools.* Clevedon: Multilingual Matters.

5. Many educators, such as Eithne Gallagher, argue that classroom teachers can also do much to promote first languages through what she terms 'interlingual classrooms' (see Gallagher 2008: chapter 5) where teachers and students can value, appreciate and understand other languages through their use in the classroom.

6. Custance, B. (2006): ESL students: changing and re-shaping identities (identities under construction), in *Teaching ESL students in mainstream classrooms: language and learning across the curriculum readings.* Hindmarsh, SA: DECS Publishing.

7. Mariani, L. (1997): Teacher support and teacher challenge in promoting learner autonomy, in *Perspectives, a Journal of TESOL,* 13(2).

8. This kind of explicit pedagogy contrasts with 'weakly framed pedagogies that feature a more child centred approach and are inevitably linked to discovery learning' see Cope, B., and Kalantzis, M. (eds) (1993): *The Powers of Literacy: A Genre Approach to Teaching Writing.* London: The Falmer Press; (and) Hammond, J. (ed) (2001): *Scaffolding: teaching and learning in language and literacy education.* Newtown, New South Wales: Primary English Teaching

Association; (and) Dare, B., Custance, B., and Polias, J. (2006): *Teaching ESL students in mainstream classrooms: language and learning across the curriculum*. Hindmarsh SA: DECS Publishing. This is not arguing for a totally teacher centred approach but for appropriate intervention: with direct teaching at certain times and more student centred teaching at others.

9. Hammond, J. (ed) (2001): *Scaffolding: teaching and learning in language and literacy education*. Newtown, New South Wales: Primary English Teaching Association.

10. Halliday, M.A.K. (1975): *Learning how to mean: explorations in the development of language*. London: Arnold; (and) Painter, C. (1984): *Into the mother tongue*. London: Arnold.

11. Vygotsky, L.S. (1978): *Mind in society: The development of higher psychological processes*, Cole, M., Steiner, V.J., Scribner, S., and Souberman, E. (Eds). Cambridge, MA: Harvard University Press; (and) Bruner, J. S. (1985): Vygotsky: A historical and conceptual perspective, in *Culture, Communication and Cognition: Vygotskian Perspectives*, Wertsch, J. (ed). Cambridge, MA: Cambridge University Press.

12. Edwards, J. (2001): *Learning, thinking and assessment*, retrieved from (27 October 2008) the website of The Tasmanian Educational Leaders' Institute: www.discover.tased.edu.au/science/conastaLTandA.htm

13. Candlin, C., and Mercer, N. (2001): *English Language Teaching in Its Social Context*, London: Routledge.

14. Veel, R. (1999): Language in school mathematics, in *Pedagogy and the shaping of consciousness: Linguistic and social processes*, Christie, F. (ed). London: Cassell. pp191-192

15. Sinclari, J.M.H., and Coulthard, M. (1975): *Towards an Analysis of Discourse: The English Used by Teachers and Pupils*. Oxford: Oxford University Press; (and) Mehan, H. (1979): *Learning Lessons: Social Organization in the Classroom*. Cambridge, MA: Harvard University Press; (and) Edwards and Mercer as cited in Gibbons, P. (2002): *Scaffolding Language, Scaffolding Learning: Teaching Second Language Learners in the Mainstream Classroom*. Portsmouth, NH: Heinemann.

16. Mercer, N. (2001): 'A language for teaching a language', in *English language teaching in its social context: a reader*, Candlin, C., and Mercer, N. (eds). London: Routledge, p245.

17. A more detailed description of this teacher working with her students can be found in Dansie, B. (2001): Scaffolding oral language: *The Hungry Giant* retold, in *Scaffolding: teaching and learning in language and literacy education*. Hammond, J. (ed.). Newtown, New South Wales: Primary English Teaching Association, chapter 4.

18. Gibbons, P. (2002): *Scaffolding language, scaffolding learning: teaching second language learners in the mainstream classroom*. Portsmouth, NH: Heinemann, chapter 4.

19. *ibid*, p15

20. Gray, B. (2007): *Accelerating the literacy development of Indigenous students*. Darwin: CDU Press.

21. Asking these questions assumes, of course, that all students understand the meanings of the words such as 'stage', emphasizing that the learning at any given point is contingent on what has gone on before. If there is not enough shared understanding about key words then it may mean going back a number of steps to build up those understandings.

22. In Accelerated Literacy pedagogy this is called reconceptualisation. For a very detailed example of the use of preformulation and reconceptualisation as part of a unit of work on Tim Winton's Book *Lockie Leonard* go to the following website: www.schools.nsw.edu.au/learning/7-12assessments/naplan/teachstrategies/yr2008/literacy/aboriginal_students/SS_AbSt.pdf

23. Gibbons, P. (2002): *Scaffolding language, scaffolding learning: teaching second language learners in the mainstream classroom.* Portsmouth, NH: Heinemann, pp17-18.

24. Here the word redundancy is used to mean that we need to make similar meanings about something so that students have more than one opportunity to take in that meaning. Here 'repetition is good' where in other contexts this may not be the case and saying that something is redundant can mean that something is superfluous.

25. Pauline Gibbons' (2002) chapter 2 is an excellent resource here, not only because it describes the various group and pair activities but also because she provides a clear rationale for using these activities within the context of the curriculum topics under focus.

26. A jigsaw activity is one where you might divide the class into four groups A, B, C and D, giving them some task to complete. Once the task is complete the students will form into different groups, each with an A, a B a C and a D, and use the information they have gained to complete a new task.

27. This teaching learning cycle now appears in various forms but it had its origins in the work of Joan Rothery initially at the North Sydney Demonstration School and was taken up by Jim Martin and others as part of the Disadvantaged Schools Program in the late 1980s in Sydney.

28. Cope, B., and Kalantzis, M. (eds) (1993): *The Powers of Literacy: A Genre Approach to Teaching Writing.* London: The Falmer Press; (and) Hammond, J. (ed) (2001): *Scaffolding: teaching and learning in language and literacy education.* Newtown, New South Wales: Primary English Teaching Association; (and) Dare, B., Custance, B., and Polias, J. (2006): *Teaching ESL students in mainstream classrooms: language and learning across the curriculum.* Hindmarsh SA: DECS Publishing.

29. See the following excellent resources which are free to download at: www.bosnsw-k6.nsw.edu.au/english/english_index.html

    Board of Studies NSW (2000): *Teaching about Texts.* Sydney: Board of Studies New South Wales.

    Board of Studies NSW (1998): *English K-6 Syllabus.* Sydney: Board of Studies New South Wales.

Chapter 7

ICT in the PYP

Greg Curtis and Jason Cone

There are few educational issues with so much unfulfilled potential over the past 15-plus years as the role of technology in the classroom. Schools and curricular frameworks have struggled with the ways in which ICT can become embedded within the educational environment in meaningful ways and to bring about substantial enhancements in student learning. The Primary Years Programme has not been immune to these challenges.

To fulfill its potential, ICT needs to be understood as a catalyst and an enabler for the type of learning envisioned. PYP has structures involving inquiry and transdisciplinary skills that can be greatly enhanced by the use of technology, but it has not clearly articulated ICT's role in this environment. Therefore, technology is certainly being used, but too often for shallow or lower-order pedagogical purposes. The mere presence of computers in the classroom or, indeed, children in front of computers, does not guarantee that technology is being used in a meaningful way to help bring about the kinds of learning needed in the 21st century.

How then can PYP schools and practitioners help to bridge this gap? How can the PYP itself lend more guidance and support for this lingering educational dilemma? There are several existing models, such as Route 21[1] and NETS,[2] that the PYP and its schools can use to develop a clear framework that enables the use of ICT to support true inquiry and 21st century learning. It is essential that such a framework is developed so that the full supportive and, indeed, transformative nature of digital learning can be leveraged for our students.

Articulating the use of ICT

The simple act of 'Googling' is, in reality, a low-order skill. Anyone can do it, but it's what you do after you click the search button that is important. Anyone, in our students' generation, can put together a PowerPoint presentation or present a digital image. But, this is simply the automation of communication. It does not mine the huge potential and necessity for digital-aged communication skills to inform, persuade and move people in a media-saturated world.

Technology's potential to support key ideas and skills is significant. It can provide easy access to primary sources to drive exploration and creative thinking, serve as a platform for true collaboration, create an environment for 'idea testing', and allow students to engage in real-life information and data handling experience. Effective use of ICT can lead to the development and refinement of problem-solving approaches, integrate design technology-like approaches to assist with hands-on inquiry, and enhance communication to real audiences. Just as most other sectors of society have harnessed technology to enhance the achievement of their goals in very real ways, so too, finally, must education.

Many studies and research papers point to the need for a strong and well-articulated goal for the use of technology in order for machines to truly support the dynamic nature of learning. Otherwise, the adoption and meaningful integration of technology can suffer. The use of technology can become haphazard, based on individual initiative, go in various directions and even bring about negative influences on the learning process.

The PYP, in its implementation guide *Making the PYP Happen,*[3] relegates the use of IT to the following passage:

> 'In the PYP, information and communication technology (ICT) is not identified as a particular subject area, but is recognized as a tool that facilitates learning throughout the curriculum.'

While, in essence, this is an appropriate role for technology (as opposed to existing as a subject area), the promise of technology to truly support the high learning ideals of the PYP could be missed. Through the rest of *Making the PYP Happen*, ICT is referred to either as a simple conduit for accessing information or a communication tool. And, to be fair, the PYP is not the only approach that is challenged with embracing an authentic and valuable role for ICT in modern, progressive ways of learning.

The PYP is a framework built on the premise that guided inquiry will lead to student learning and spiraling understanding. Yet, the role of technology in facilitating this positive force of inquiry is thinly articulated, or perhaps even misunderstood. The use of technology as a catalyst for deep inquiry and not simply 'researching a question' is somewhat lost in the PYP literature. This literature *hints* at a huge role for ICT, suggesting that practitioners think of ways in which ICT is envisioned as a catalyst and enabler of this type of learning, yet this leveraging of technology is not well-supported.

Spotlight 1: ICT in PYP inquiry and communication

In a grade 4 unit on poetry, students explored different styles of poetry writing and other forms of creative expression. They investigated the lives and background of favorite poets using the internet. Students then created original works of art, took digital photos, and selected accompanying music to create a video montage of images set to music and their own voice in the background reading the poem. The finished product was published on the student's blog for feedback.

In a unit on art and artists, students explore the life and art of an artist of their choice. They create original works of art in the same style as their artist, visit museums to see original works by their artist. Students then create an online three-dimensional virtual art gallery with their own art and selected examples from their artist. The gallery includes a guided/narrated tour for visitors. Links to the museum 'spaces' are published on the school website and classroom blogs where visitors can post comments and questions that students respond to throughout the year.

These are examples of the kinds of ICT-supported experiences to help facilitate inquiry and the ability to communicate the outcomes of this inquiry in novel and impactful ways. But, the impetus has historically been up to the individual school or teacher.

ICT and transdisciplinary inquiry

One of the main tenets of the PYP is the explicit inclusion of transdisciplinary skills and themes into the programme. There are many ways in which we can align the use of technology to the aims of this curriculum, including transdisciplinary learning and the attainment of key concepts. However, as mentioned above, this is currently left largely to the initiative of the practitioner. In other words, teachers are left on their own, not only to decide how to use ICT, but also how to 'flag' its use in support of key elements of the PYP.

Technology can provide real world enablers for the PYP transdisciplinary approach. Like many concepts, this transdisciplinary approach must be operationalised in order for it to impact positively on student learning. It must make the important journey from concept to practice. In fact, it has been our observation that many PYP teachers seem to struggle with ways to take this important transdisciplinary element of the program and enact it within their units. The potential of ICT to provide a powerful way in which to assist in the 'doing' of transdisciplinary skills should be articulated and supported within a framework.

Spotlight 2: Thinking, social, communication, self-management and research skills

Grade 3 students use a variety of technologies to develop speaking, listening and presentation skills. Students view videos online of presenters and story tellers. Students use digital cameras to record each other and themselves reading stories, and storytelling in different styles and genres. After capturing the original video files, students use digital video editing software to create short movie clips that demonstrate qualities of effective speaking and listening. As part of the assessment process students view and reflect on their own and others' videos. Students then transfer these skills to the presentation they prepare and deliver to their class and the school as a summative assessment in their unit of inquiry.

Embedding ICT in a larger model of inquiry

When positioned properly as a central enabler, technology can help to elevate the tasks that we design for students. Project- and problem-based learning provide structures to leverage the use of technology and enhance the learning of our students. Of course, these approaches could be used without technology, but their potential would be greatly diminished.

'Reinventing the project approach doesn't mean discarding the venerable model. Rather, we advocate that building on what we already know is what is good about project-based learning. By maximising the use of digital tools to reach essential learning goals, teachers can overcome the boundaries and limitations of the traditional classroom. Some tools open new windows onto student thinking, setting the stage for more productive classroom conversations. Still others allow for instant global connections, redefining the meaning of a learning community. When teachers thoughtfully integrate these tools, the result is like a 'turbo boost' that can take project-based learning into a new orbit.'[4]

More authentic, student-influenced and differentiated forms of assessment are available to teachers through technology. Students can now synthesise and transfer their learning in a myriad of ways before it is communicated (through a myriad of media) to authentic audiences around the world. These are learning artifacts for the 21st century and, by engaging in the media-rich world in which they live *outside* of school, a level of higher-order authenticity can become the norm in students' demonstration of their growing understanding.

What better way to develop a global outlook than by engaging with the world beyond the classroom in meaningful ways? How better to understand systems than by learning within one?

The PYP is aligned with many current pedagogical trends and ways of thinking, many of which have embedded the use of technology within their practical applications in ways that the PYP can draw from. It is consistent with many of the aspects of Understanding by Design and is a conceptual cousin to other established movements. The impetus to make greater and more focused use of ICT is not just driven by new possibilities in learning, but also the nature of the rapidly changing world around us. While the technology tools we use are bound to change over time, the need to infuse technology into the learning environment in a transformative way will always be with us.

As mentioned above, problem-based and project-based learning (PBL) are approaches that have enjoyed certain prominence within the changing educational landscape over the past number of years. These PBLs support the kind of inquiry and transdisciplinary thinking that is at the heart of the PYP. Also, these approaches heavily support the inclusion of ICT as a major catalyst and enabler in a learning environment that seeks to develop students' abilities to apply and transfer what they have learned within new environments and contexts.

'Project-based learning – powered by contemporary technologies – is a strategy certain to turn traditional classrooms upside down. When students learn by engaging in real world projects, nearly every aspect of their experience changes. Instead of following the teacher's lead, learners pursue their own questions to create their own meaning.'[5] Does this not mirror some of the goals of the PYP exhibition?

Spotlight 3: The PYP exhibition

The PYP exhibition provides an excellent opportunity for IT integration in the context of project- or problem-based learning. The internet provides instant access to information, current issues and global perspectives as well as the ability for students of all ages to engage with real people on real issues that they find compelling. Grade 5 students independently select an issue that has personal, local and global significance to them. Students work with mentors, teachers, and other students to develop goals, timelines and action plans for their project.

Throughout the entire process the use of technology creates an ongoing trail/archive of each individual's particular path for the duration of the learning experience. Students periodically examine and reflect on their learning and ultimately get a deeper understanding about how they learn. Student reflection is also documented and published using a variety of digital media that allows peers, teachers, mentors, and others to provide constructive feedback and questions.

Authentic assessment

Like the embedded use of technology, schools have struggled with authentic assessment for a very long time. Simply put, authentic assessment is the process of creating assessment tasks which allow students to demonstrate their deep and growing understanding through the completion of tasks. These tasks require the application and transference of skills and knowledge taught as part of the curriculum. In parallel, it is also a process of looking for authentic evidence of learning in the products and performances of our students.

'Understanding is revealed in performance. Understanding is revealed as transferability of core ideas, knowledge, and skill, on challenging tasks in a variety of contexts. Thus, assessment for understanding must be grounded in authentic performance-based tasks.'[6]

The use of technology in this essential process is clear. Technology can be viewed as a performance task enabler when viewed within the context of demonstrating student understanding.

Spotlight 4: Authentic Assessment

'The children are becoming aware that real problems require solutions based on the integration of knowledge that spans and connects several subject areas.'

Quote from a PYP teacher

Grade 5 students in Switzerland gather local data on climate trends and glacial melting. Students post ongoing findings on a collaborative web space (blog/wiki) and invite other schools to share data and reflect on possible causes. Students engage in online discussions, and work in virtual collaborative groups, with representatives from different schools in each group to propose and share possible solutions.

For the final assessment students propose and present recommended actions to the local school community, administration and school board that eventually result in a change of school policy. Students then reflect on the entire process of initiating change and publish this on the school website as well as their collaborative blog. Among other things, the use of IT provides an invaluable tool in authentic assessment and is a driving force in 'doing science'.

21st century skills: a larger context

The PYP need not undertake the daunting task of developing its own framework for the use of ICT and, by extension, an approach that acknowledges the importance of an emerging set of skills and approaches to learning. Many groups have dedicated themselves to helping to define these frameworks.

Much excellent work has been produced in the past number of years around the notion of the changing needs and realities to be served by schools. For example, The Partnership for 21st Century Skills was established in 2002 with the stated mission to: 'Serve as a catalyst to position 21st century skills at the center of US K-12 education by building collaborative partnerships among education, business, community and government leaders.'[7]

Technology is a key component of this approach. Recently, the Partnership unveiled an approach to 21st century learning, called Route 21. This approach outlines ways in which technology (among other approaches) can support 21st century learning and, by extension, many of the central tenets of the PYP. Route 21 seeks to outline the needs of 21st century learning around facets including learning and innovation skills; information, media and technology skills; life and career skills; and core subjects with 21st century themes.[8] Apple has also formulated an excellent overview of this environment, called Apple Classrooms for Tomorrow – Today (or ACOT2).[9]

The benefit of adopting an approach such as Route 21 or ACOT2 is that it supplies a context for the use of technology which is *larger* than technology itself. The PYP couches the acquisition of skills and knowledge within a context that is larger than these skills and knowledge goals are, in and of themselves. UbD, too, makes it quite clear that knowledge and skills acquisition must service deep understanding and transfer. ICT must also service something larger than itself.

We cannot, as we used to, simply use technology to learn about technology. The shift of the International Society for Technology in Education's (ISTE) standards from their 'machine-focus' of several years ago to their renewed commitment to broader 21st century skills is evidence of that. So, too, is the recent iteration of the American Association of School Librarians' 'Standards for the 21st Century Learners'.[10] It is clear that the focus for many is on the future (or at least the present) and that a structured approach for the place of ICT in that future is essential.

Too often, technology is a 'free floater' in schools and is not focused on serving a greater purpose. The greater purpose can be found in some of the central tenets of both the PYP and the approaches espoused by Route 21, *etc.* If technology is properly positioned to serve these larger goals, it can find a focus and a worthy role in learning. A framework supporting such explicit applications of technology is needed by any educational programme, including the PYP.

When ICT is properly embedded or infused within curricular areas in relevant and meaningful ways, it can enhance teaching and learning and serve as a catalyst for communication, collaboration, creativity, inquiry, global awareness, and other 21st century skills.

Spotlight 5: collaboration, inquiry and problem-solving

Grade 4 students studying space exploration and general laws of physics set up a web-based discussion forum and engage in dialogue about Newton's laws of motion. A NASA scientist joins the forum and students discuss Newton's laws in the context of space exploration. Students also inquire about other areas of space exploration.

Kindergarten students (EC) use computer programs to create commands to control virtual animals, cars, and spaceships to navigate through various visual environments. Once students have mastered the commands and controls of the computer-based object, they transfer this knowledge to small programmable robots that they must program or command to physically navigate through real obstacle courses and mazes. To assess students' understanding and transfer of skills and knowledge, students work individually and in small groups to solve problems they encounter while programming virtual objects and programmable robots.

Friedman comments meaningfully:

'For my money, they could engrave (this) on the doorway of every school in America: Nobody works harder at learning than a curious kid. Some kids are just born that way, but for the many who are not, the best way to make kids love learning is either to instill in them a sense of curiosity, by great teaching, or stimulate their own innate curiosity by making available to them all the technologies of the flat-world platform so they can educate themselves in an enormously rich way.'[11]

Let's hope that the answer lies in both great teaching and in the use of these technologies.

The recently-revised NETS standards are a good example of an existing structure that could be used by PYP schools in helping to focus their approach to the use of technology to enhance learning. This set of standards (there are individual standards for students, teachers and administrators) blends well with 21st century approaches espoused by Route 21, the George Lucas Foundation's Edutopia[12] and other groups. All of these groups focus on similar needs for the future.

The importance of creativity, collaboration, problem-solving, and communication, are examples of these commonalities. The NETS standards highlight the need to move away from focusing on technology as a means to learn about technology. Instead, it helps ensure that we use technology to leverage crucial aspects such as creativity, collaboration and citizenship.

Certainly, this idea of using technology for more than learning about technology is not new. It has been espoused by many in the field of ICT and education for years.

But, we seldom see it enacted effectively. The trick, we believe, is to move the discussion out of the ICT realm and into the curricular realm. The decisions we need to make and the actions we need to take are not about technology, but about learning.

Route 21 and NETS allow teachers and schools to use ICT to address these 21st century skills beyond the keyboard. NETS articulates the role of ICT as a vehicle to address many of the attributes valued by the PYP. Ideas of 21st century learning lean heavily on the concept of what we call 'the shift in orders'. The mechanical integration of technology will lead to nothing but more mechanics. Finding information is now a low order skill and definitely not the end game of inquiry.

As Daniel Pink points out, 'story', or narrative, is one of the six senses needed in the conceptual age. How do we help students turn inquiry and experience into powerful narratives of various forms using ICT? This is an example of this 'shift in orders' ... as mentioned, finding information is not a high order skill, but creating a narrative that makes sense of that information and appeals to people is part of the 'new' high order.

Guidance for teachers

NETS teacher and administrator standards also provide a guide as to what sort of engagement practitioners must have with technology in order to leverage it properly within a modern learning context. A relatively simple way for the PYP to provide the kind of direction and guidance that teachers and schools need to use ICT effectively would be to adopt frameworks such as Route 21 and/or the NETS standards.

Technology is involved in a symbiotic dance with change. Technology can impact lives, but changes in sensibilities, priorities, global dynamics, *etc*, also impact technology. Basing a program solely on current technology and mechanical application of that technology is not going to work. Change is the only constant. We cannot future-proof against changes in technology, but we can develop an approach to the use of technology that can adapt to inevitable changes. If our focus is on true inquiry and higher-order skills, these will not be dependent upon changes in technology. We 'simply' adjust our tool kit to take advantage of new or changed tools and environments. But, if the framework for using technology is static, it will always become a race to keep up.

This also demands a change in our thinking about what constitutes critical learning. The PYP, in many ways, reinforces current thinking that emphasises concept, idea and skill over static content knowledge. There is a chorus of voices in the world of academic research and progressive thought, singing a similar tune. As Daniel Pink says:

> '[O]ver time, we moved from the Agricultural Age to the Industrial Age to the Information Age. The latest instance of this pattern is today's transition from the Information Age to the Conceptual Age once again fed by affluence (the abundance that characterizes western life), technological progress (the automation of several kinds of white-collar work), and globalization (certain types of knowledge work moving to Asia).

'In short, we've progressed from a society of farmers to a society of factory workers to a society of knowledge workers. And now we're progressing yet again – to a society of creators and empathizers, of pattern recognizers and meaning makers.'[13]

Howard Gardner believes that we've lost the ability to engage with learning as a *discipline*:

'Why, despite the best motivated efforts, do so many students continue to adhere to erroneous or inadequate ways of thinking? A major reason, I believe, is that neither teachers nor students nor policymakers nor ordinary citizens sufficiently appreciate the differences between *subject matter* and *discipline*. ...A discipline constitutes a distinctive way of thinking about the world. Scientists observe the world; come up with tentative classifications, concepts, and theories; design experiments in order to test these tentative theories; revise the theories in light of the findings; and then return, newly informed, to make further observations, redo classifications, and devise experiments. ...[H]istorians attempt to reconstruct the past from scattered and often contradictory fragments of information, mostly written, but increasingly supported by graphic, film, or oral testimony.'[14]

The role of technology in creating an environment based on the authentic 'doing' of a discipline is clear. Do scientists and historians work and continue to learn without technology? Of course not, but ICT's role in their work is both infused and directed by a purpose.

But, how much are we prepared to leverage ICT to reinforce this shift? Without a meaningful approach and guidance for teachers in the use of technology, how can practitioners turn the corner in their practice and truly engage students in central PYP learning?

ICT as professional enabler

We have steered away from another topic, namely the need to provide ICT tools for professionals, which is beyond the scope of this chapter. Technology as an enabler for professional learning communities and its role in effective curriculum mapping should also be supported by the PYP. Think of the possibilities of an online curriculum mapping system that allows teachers to develop PYP units and easily draw from an articulated set of ICT 'intersections' to help with technology infusion. What about the ability to map effective ICT use with transdisciplinary themes/skills and the learner profile? Intelligent application of such tools has the potential to help the PYP to enact the very best of its pedagogical approach.

Conclusions

We have argued for, or at least hinted at, a few key principles that we feel must be addressed. These can be summarised as:

 • The use of technology in mechanistic ways, or as a mere automator of tasks, must stop.

- The use of ICT must be placed within a larger context in order to serve the school's learning goals. This context should draw on the large body of work surrounding the 21st century movement.

- Practitioners must seek meaningful ways to infuse ICT as a central part of the learning environment.

- Practitioners must be supported by schools and organisations that seek to illustrate the role of ICT in addressing interdisciplinary themes/skills and the IB learner profile. Connections between the promise of ICT and the central philosophy of the PYP must be made explicit.

- The PYP structures of curriculum development and documentation must provide entry points for the authentic use of technology to serve these goals.

Throughout this chapter, we have tried to show some of the uses of technology to support the aims and objectives of the PYP. The thoughtful application of technology can help schools and teachers to achieve many of the programme's central tenets. Technology can help to bridge the gap between the conceptual underpinnings of the PYP and its implementation within the real learning environment. In order to do so, we must ask some essential questions. In 2009, for example, how can a student exhibit the traits of the IB learner profile without the thoughtful use of technology?

In recent work we have defined '21st century learning' as being characterised by various approaches (project learning, social and emotional learning, comprehensive assessment, integrated learning and technology infusion), to service important 21st century skills (creativity/innovation, inquiry/critical thinking/problem-solving, communication/collaboration, global thinking and leadership/responsibility).[15]

This focus was drawn from the work of Route 21 and Edutopia and influenced by many recent writings on the topic. Perhaps it also serves as an example of how education can attempt to find a context that includes ICT as a central approach in attaining its learning goals. ICT as an interloper in learning environments, wandering in and out with little direction, has not helped students to learn in the 21st century.

Technology must be infused throughout the PYP framework, either through an existing model or one devised by the IB itself. The links that ICT can support, such as between libraries, information literacy, 21st century skills and interdisciplinary skills, should become a central part of the programme.

The PYP is currently in use in hundreds of schools around the world. These schools look to the IB for leadership in many areas. Teachers look to the PYP to help them with the complex task of delivering an effective programme which is true to the intent of the framework.

New ways of thinking about learning in the 21st century provide both an urgency and an avenue to change the environment of our schools. It's an exciting time and there seems to be a convergence of voices pointing to similar shifts and needs. The role of technology in this shift is clear, and yet its potential can only be realized through a directed and explicit approach to ICT's role in the learning process.

References

1. www.21stcenturyskills.org/route21

2. www.iste.org/AM/Template.cfm?Section=NETS

3. International Baccalaureate Organization, (2007): *Making the PYP happen.* Cardiff: IBO, p11

4. Boss, S., and Krauss, J. (2008): *Reinventing Project-Based Learning: Your Field Guide to Real-World Projects in the Digital Age.* Washington: International Society for Technology in Education, p12.

5. *ibid*, p11.

6. Wiggins, G., and McTighe, J. (2005): *Understanding by Design* (2nd edition). Alexandria, Virginia: ASCD, p153.

7. www.21stcenturyskills.org/

8. Route 21 – Framework Flyer
www.21stcenturyskills.org/documents/framework_flyer_updated_jan_09_final-1.pdf

9. http://newali.apple.com/acot2/program.shtml

10. www.ala.org/

11. Friedman, T.L. (2006): T*he World is Flat: A Brief History of the Twenty-first Century* (Release 2.0). New York: Farrar, Straus and Giroux, p304.

12. www.edutopia.org/

13. Pink, D.H. (2006): *A Whole New Mind: Why Right-Brainers Will Rule the Future.* New York: Riverhead Books, pp49-50.

14. Gardner, H. (2007): *Five Minds for the Future.* Boston: Harvard Business School Press, pp27-28.

15. Greg Curtis, International School of Beijing, 2008.

Chapter 8

Actions speak louder than words

Simon Davidson

After I drafted out an outline for this book, I passed it round a few colleagues for feedback. After some early positive comments, I started to feel a little too self-satisfied. Then Paul Morris[1] pointed out that many schools find the Action component of the PYP difficult. I had to agree. I had come across good examples of action in many PYP schools, but it didn't appear to be done well with any consistency.

I resolved to find an expert to write a chapter on Action in the PYP, someone who had perfected it. I did some research, and found many great examples of action in PYP schools throughout the world. There were plenty of grandiose events we could be proud of. I had seen many examples of small actions in a classroom, when children made good choices about how to behave with each other. Often they didn't realise they were naturally carrying out the action component.

Unfortunately, I didn't find an expert with all the answers – perhaps I didn't look hard enough. However, as I looked, and thought through what I was looking for, I came to the conclusion that the most important part of PYP action is daily classroom practice, although this is perhaps not always made explicit enough.

Therefore I introduce the terms *big actions* and *everyday actions*. Big actions are large-scale projects that can be impressive, and can leave a deep impression on children. However, in schools which are already busy, it is unrealistic to add them very regularly. Therefore considerable power also comes in encouraging good daily choices to turn into age-appropriate daily actions. Smaller *everyday actions* can provide ongoing reflection and develop deeply-embedded pattern of thought and action.

We have to be realistic about young children's necessarily restricted spheres of influence. However we can tap into their passionate sense of fairness to develop responsibility within these spheres, with the habit of acting on thoughtful choices. Then they will be well on their way to becoming global citizens who live out the learner profile as adults.

Action: global citizens living out their learning

To understand the action component, we need to consider two aspects: socially responsible attitudes and ways of thinking, and the ability to act these out in their own lives.[2]

The former is central to all IB programmes, which seek to develop global citizens who will play their part in society. This is summarised in two lists of attributes:

The **learner profile**: inquirers, knowledgeable, thinkers, communicators, principled, open-minded, caring, risk-takers, balanced, reflective;[3]

and **PYP attitudes**: appreciation, commitment, confidence, cooperation, creativity, curiosity, empathy, enthusiasm, independence, integrity, respect, and tolerance.[4]

Scanning these attributes gives a clear idea of the morally articulate and ethical people who should arise from IB schools: they are knowledgeable and thoughtful about the world. They are caring and principled, and become adults with commitment, empathy, and integrity. They develop a service orientation to enrich their communities, in their school community, and the local or global community they live in as an adult.

These attributes are developed with a connected approach that is one of the key strengths, and also main challenges, of the PYP. As with the transdisciplinary approach to learning, values and attitudes are not separated into distinct lessons, but taught with a coherent and integrated approach.

Rather than learning consisting of isolated 'book exercises', children learn to apply their learning to their lives as a matter of course. They connect their thinking by applying skills, concepts and insights from many areas to complex situations. We want them to develop both as enduring understandings and enduring patterns of life. Thus action is not an extra or separate element after normal learning, but its integral conclusion.

Overcome one's limitations

Education has a central role in helping students overcome the limitations of their life circumstances. When children come from underprivileged backgrounds, they need to be presented with rich examples of human potential to which they can aspire. They need to experience taking action which shows that they can make a difference.

Those who worked in privileged schools in rich parts of the world have a different problem. Students may be internationally very diverse, but are often from a narrow socioeconomical range, also providing a limited view of the world. Such students have to understand and appreciate their privileged nature, and have responsibility without paternalistic attitudes, so that they can play a responsible role with more socio-economically diverse communities throughout the globe. Their awareness can be developed through suitable Who We Are and Sharing The Planet units.

Appropriate attitudes and a sense of responsibility can be a challenge in such schools. One occasionally comes across children who have learnt that someone else will care for them, so they are not very concerned about leaving homework or musical instruments at home, or who pay no regard to picking up after themselves. This isn't a cognitive difficulty, but embedded non-PYP attitudes. One can't overcome this by having a bake sale, but by daily acceptance of personal responsibility that creates suitable attitudes. In other words, by paying serious attention to everyday actions with appropriate reflection, until students develop self-awareness and take responsibility.

Choose, act, reflect components

PYP action has three components: choose, act, reflect.[5] Students choose an appropriate action, actually do it, and reflect on its efficacy. These are often referred to as a cycle: this reflection may lead to new choices and the cycle begins again. This can be misleading, as it implies that reflection is a separate stage that only happens after action. However, it is also a process that happens continually during *choice* and *action* stages.

Making meaningful choices

It is important that children learn to make good choices, to think for themselves and take responsibility in an age-appropriate and realistic way. Actions only have an enduring impact when they affect a student's inner conviction, which requires genuine choice and genuine responsibility. Remember that our students are generally great at telling us what we want to hear. They easily pick up teachers' choices and say them back to them, without really passing it through their brain. Passive choices are unlikely to be sustained in school or beyond it.

Meaningful choices imply meaningful responsibility, without coercion. This doesn't leave us powerless. We can frame the choice and make sure that students make it carefully. Before students can make a choice, they have to think it through. (Perhaps reflection should actually be the first element.)

We identify situations requiring choice and action. These may be social issues which may arise in the class, such as some children being left out in the playground, or bullying. Children may face choices about healthy eating. Perhaps they don't put their books away or pick up after themselves.

Then we help children identify the issues involved and reach a conclusion. This may take time, as children have to think through the issue themselves before making their choice. Education takes time to have profound and lasting results. Students may learn more from making a bad choice and reflecting, than from having a good choice imposed upon them. Two possible choices are often overlooked:

• No action – as a positive choice, not a default.

• The action of learning more, to understand what the situation is all about. It is often appropriate to concentrate on becoming *thinkers, inquirers,* and *knowledgeable.* Then students have something to say when an issue comes up, and a basis for intelligent action.

Often children and adults are not conscious of their choices. One approach to changing is to make choices explicit, and think them through, and hope that this affects the implicit choices. Sometimes, however, it is better to start with trying other patterns of behaviour, developing an implicit 'feel' for this other behaviour, and then talking through when students already have a 'feel' for both types of behaviour. Even the most dedicated teacher can't do this all the time. We'd love it if all students chose to tidy the room and carry out end-of-day jobs perfectly. Some actions may not always be student-initiated – but they just need to be done anyway.

Acting – make it a habit

Do student choices automatically lead to *student-initiated action*? Not necessarily. It is important not to gloss over the second element, act. This is anything but trivial. Personally, I have to admit to regular problems turning good choices into actions. I decide to clean the car, but put it off. I resolve to exercise more, but don't get round to it. I choose to write more regularly, to eat less junk food, and to do more household chores, but I don't always actually do so. This is a profound aspect of action that many of us do badly in our own lives. As the saying goes: 'The road to hell is paved with good intentions.'

The more students develop the habit of carrying through on their good choices the better. We want students to develop the habit of actually acting on their choices. They can become the people who subconsciously tidy the room without thinking, who help friends automatically.

One of the difficulties of concentrating on inspiring one-off actions is that students don't learn to carry through their choices long-term. It can be easier to carry through something unusual and novel than to carry through something easier when the novelty factor wears off.

Facilitating reflection

We often set up a formal process where children fill in reflection forms. These can be useful occasionally to highlight particular aspects of the reflection process, but quickly become artificial and tiresome if they are overused. This becomes counter-productive for students, who learn how to fill in formulaic responses that teachers will accept. Remember that reflection is a habit of mind. Hopefully, as adults we reflect on what we are doing throughout the day, even if we rarely write it out. Occasionally even writing reflections at the end of units of inquiry can become disconnected from daily professional reflection, and thus becomes an additional chore, rather than a tool for improving teaching and learning.

Rather than focusing on a paper product, it may be better to concentrate on developing a disposition of reflection, and making it progressively deeper and more embedded in students' thinking. This requires consistently talking through students' actions. The actual effect isn't the criteria for success. Rather students can develop a greater awareness of cause and effect, and a set of values that get embedded in their peer culture.

Reflection also needs to be future-oriented, focused on guiding future action rather than placing blame for past actions. We are developing students who help each other improve, rather than moaning about difficulties or revelling in blaming others. It can be more effective to have many short discussions very regularly, focusing on whatever choices and actions children are currently involved in. The teacher can be a catalyst to student talk, a *provocateur* for the students' own thoughts in quick reflections: Is the room clear? How do you feel about what you did? How do you think (name) feels?

Alternatively, reflections may be a series of longer discussions about actions in a particular unit of inquiry, or about a major class issue that has caught the students' attention. As with many other aspects of learning, the teacher's role is to become unnecessary over time. Students develop the habit of thinking through implications. Reflection becomes internalised. Children ask themselves 'was that a good choice?' This is an excellent investment of teacher time, which will be regained later on if children self-regulate their actions. We hope that they will continue to reflect and discuss amongst themselves as children get older and they become less willing to talk through significant issues with adults.

Everyday actions and big actions

Because the power of actions can involve developing a service disposition on a daily basis, I introduce the following terms:

- Big actions: the occasional grandiose acts that can make a substantial impact. By their nature they are exceptional, and challenging. These tend to be group actions, often initiated by a sub-group of students. It is wonderful when students spontaneously initiate them, but don't worry when they don't.

- Everyday actions: these should be an ongoing part of classroom life for all students, and will include individual, as well as group and class, actions.

Compare this with reading. An author's visit can have a big impact on students. It is a wonderful bonus, but you don't abandon your reading programme. Students need daily interaction with texts to become fluent readers. Similarly, they need daily choices, actions and reflection to become fluent in global citizenship. However, occasional special action events can be highly significant for students.

Everyday actions

Everyday action should be a key part of school life. Primary children may not be able to 'save the world'. That's quite hard when you are eight. It's not easy as an adult, either. The more we focus on issues outside children's spheres of influence, the more we highlight their powerlessness. If we develop their character dispositions and ability to carry through on their choices, they can have a significant impact on the world later in life.

It is better to consider what children experience directly and what they can affect directly. This is mainly within their families and classrooms, and around the school and playgrounds – their 'spheres of influence'. Such areas are often profoundly significant to young children, and draw on their feelings about fairness and justice. As students mature their sphere of influence will expand. The more they have reflected, the more they will be aware of what they can affect and how, so they are empowered to make good choices.

Similarly, our students don't leave the PYP able to solve differential equations, but we have done the groundwork for them to do so later. No Nobel Prizes have yet been awarded to primary science projects but PYP students do, we hope, develop the fundamental scientific ways of thinking and some will become great scientists in the future. We have a great formative period for habits of mind and attitudes, and initiating global awareness, which become an enduring part of their lives.

Big actions

At their best, big actions can be life-defining events for students, as they set out on their earnest missions to save humanity. Children will have many strong emotions, usually individual age-appropriate and circumstance-appropriate responses. Students of all ages have taken their first steps to help a community by raising funds in very traditional ways, including bake sales. If we help them develop commitment and carry-through, this can sow the seeds for much great global citizenship in adulthood.

Sometimes it is hard to channel children's passionate reaction to major events and natural disasters. Perhaps the readers will recognise this situation. A student mentions a problem they have seen on television, or talked about at home. "Isn't x a problem!" Everyone agrees. They feel bad about it and they have well-developed empathy. Someone says: "We need to do something!" They all think about recent models. Perhaps bake sales, raffles, and sponsored events.

The class gets in a frenzy of poster making. They put up posters everywhere that fire regulations forbid, and conveniently forget to reflect on their environmental impact. They pester parents to spend money on ingredients, and then bake with them. Everyone gives up healthy eating to have the tasty cakes (I like that part).

The timetable is disrupted once more, crumbs line the corridor, but children are proud that they have collected nearly as much as parents spent on ingredients. Many children learned how to organise an event and make great brownies. Some got better at pestering parents, although most were already experts. This is all good learning, but it has little connection to the underlying disaster. It takes more time, and a more reflective approach, to really investigate complex problems and try to work through the proposed solutions, none of which are normally perfect or straightforward.

Challenges of big actions

This exemplifies some of the challenges of big actions. PYP schools can be full of wonderful activities. So wonderfully full, it's hard to allocate time for reflection, yet we would like to add more activities. Perhaps you've just had a classical guitarist performing; you've spend hours writing long parent reports; you feel you have to perform a Broadway-quality production because it will be compared to the amazing performance from grade 4 last year; the librarian has booked a great children's writer; you need to keep your unit going. Choosing to add a big action implies dropping something else. So what do you leave out?

In a reflective classroom, where discourse regularly relates learning to the outside world, students will bring up global problems with no easy solution, such as dramatic natural disasters and the results of warfare. Students with a healthy sense of empathy often have an emotional response to them, but what can they do about it?

Often the event is far outside their experience, and it would take several weeks of class research to really understand the situation. Without understanding, it is difficult to have thoughtful action, and one risks encouraging thoughtless action, when actions are determined by simplistic emotional reactions. Children could do something based on their normal repertoire of action events, but we don't want to create 'busy work for the soul', without understanding. That wouldn't develop educated global citizens, but may lead to shallow adults who might not live ethically, but give a little money to charity on the side.

If there isn't time to understand the problem, no action may be the best choice. In this situation, a good choice is to learn more, considering learner profile words like *knowledgeable* and *thinkers*.

Big actions can provide excellent authentic contexts for big learning

Having said that, a little youthful naivety is healthy in energising students' commitments to tasks in which they can learn other skills. As students undertake *big actions* they often have to develop and apply a wide range of skills. They are often very enthusiastic about using mathematics to calculate funds raised. They have to use all their transdisciplinary skills as they think through the action, plan and organise themselves, and then communicate the action to the rest of the school. They need to work together, and solve all the practical problems that arise. Their learning often extends to the home when families support their student's action. They can also learn about the importance of partnership, particularly when they have to cooperate with external agencies as well as others in the school.

Often similar learning can be embedded in strong units of inquiry, but the authenticity of a significant action is great for giving students' learning a sense of purpose.

Development trips

Similar issues arise with older students. A Third World action project may be only an exotic adventure for well-travelled students who have already been round the globe several times. However it may be a chance to engage with other parts of the planet. It can be a life-changing experience for some students.

The cost is high, with as much spent on travel as on development. Rationally it is more effective to just send money to responsible agencies in the area. It is dangerous to second-guess the motives of the students, which can be very personal. It is important, however, to foster genuine and sincere motivation behind them when possible. For this a sympathetic peer or colleague needs to facilitate reflection to internalise the learning and deepen the understanding of the complexity involved in real situations.

Conclusions

Action has a central role in the PYP for making real global citizens; not those with head knowledge only, but also in developing students' personalities.

Big actions can be time-consuming and risk dealing with issues beyond students' spheres of influence and understanding. However they can also be rich learning experiences for many children. Therefore they should be included occasionally within a balanced programme.

Everyday actions can be carried out regularly. Even the smallest of choices, providing it is significant to students, can be powerful in developing habits of making thoughtful choices, and carrying them out over sustained periods of time.

When these are combined with a programme of inquiry that develops thoughtful and knowledgeable students who are empathetic to global problems, students will truly become global citizens who act on their knowledge with sensitivity and follow-through. We may not be able to measure the effect within a school year, but action-oriented students make the world a much better place, which is the true final and summative assessment of the Primary Years Programme.

References

1. Paul Morris is currently Primary Principal of the International School of Stuttgart.

2. International Baccalaureate Organization, (2007): *Making the PYP happen.* Cardiff: IBO, p25.

3. *ibid*, p4.

4. *ibid*, p24.

5. *ibid*, p24.

Chapter 9

Neuroeducation: using brain sciences to inform education

Jeb Schenck

Introduction

This chapter reviews how findings in the emerging field of neuroeducation can inform teaching and learning in PYP classrooms. I examine how students' brains process information from initial pattern detection, through how the attention and emotional systems function together, and how working memory links up to long-term memory to establish learning. Throughout, I explore the implications for learning, and for assessment based upon brain growth.

Implications of neuroeducation for all educators

Learning is a lifelong endeavor, and the brain is literally capable of learning from cradle to grave. Looking at how the brain affects education is not the latest education trend; the brain isn't likely to become unfashionable anytime soon. However, the brain is the most complex system ever studied and because of that complexity it takes combined efforts of multiple disciplines to understand it. One outcome of this combined effort is the emergence of an entire new domain called *Neuroeducation* which combines brain-based education, cognitive neurosciences, and cognitive psychology. Each of these fields provides foundational research, and together the complexities of the brain are slowly yielding their secrets.

Although learning takes place in the brain, few educators know even the rudiments of how the brain works, and consequently why some educational practices work and others fail. For centuries the practice of education has been working with the brain, all the while ignorant of the processes that govern it. Our understanding of the brain continues to grow rapidly through thousands of small steps, and by the occasional leap in discoveries, such as the pruning of neurons, decision-making areas in an adolescent's brain and mirror neurons. Now enough progress has been made that we know some of the basic processes well enough to make appropriate applications in the classroom and witness real changes in performance.

Making sense of the world: pattern detection

One of the first tasks of the brain is to make sense of a deluge of stimuli. It does so by trying to find patterns, and seeing how those patterns fit together with still other patterns. This can either project a student forward with "ah-has" of discovery, or halt them instantly in their tracks. All disciplines in education use patterns, though we are frequently not explicit in helping students recognize them. We leave the questions 'What are we looking for?' or 'Why do we want to do that?' unstated. As educators, we tend to assume students will detect the pattern, but unfortunately many students don't. If no pattern is found the brain shifts its attention away, and the student goes off task. Students become frustrated and stop working.

Supporting pattern recognition

Teachers can do a lot to help support their students to recognise patterns: explain; demonstrate; or show what pattern is being sought; and frequently check with the students to see if they know what pattern or task they are searching for. Then lead the students in finding how that pattern creates yet a larger pattern. For example, words can form a pattern of sentences (Can students decode the sentence?). Sentences make a paragraph (What was the paragraph about?). A series of paragraphs form a still larger pattern (How did the paragraphs illuminate the topic?).

Attention systems

Once a pattern is detected, our attention system in the brain focuses on it, at least for a while. Imagine a totally dark room. There are many objects scattered throughout the room, undetectable without light. Our attention system is like switching on a searchlight, and sweeping across the room. At any moment only a small part of the room is illuminated by the beam of our attention's searchlight.

At last a pattern is recognized. Perhaps it is a red chair, and we stop searching in order to process this information. Our attention systems ask: 'What is it? Where is it?' However, if too much information comes in all at once, the attention system is rapidly overwhelmed and no one thing is fixed upon. The result is that most, if not all, the information stops being thoroughly processed and is lost. If new information is not actively attended to, there is almost no chance of the information or lesson ever getting into memory and being learned.

The brain actually has several systems devoted to maintaining attention, but can only process a limited amount at a time. A famous example is the 'cocktail party effect'.[1] A common variation goes something like this. You're having a conversation with a guest at a party; nearby another couple is also talking. You overhear them saying your name and, without shifting your eyes away from your guest, you mentally shift your attention to listen to what is being said about you.

Meanwhile you say politely say, "Umm unhuh" to your guest, pretending to listen. Generally, one can't follow both the guest's comments very closely *and* the other conversation, because of the limited resources of the attention systems. The few remaining resources of the attention system are redirected to monitoring the other conversation. The limited attention system isn't able to focus adequately. Our brain shifts its mental 'searchlight' to something else that it considers to be of greater importance because it can only pay attention to a few things at once. Indeed, research suggests that we can process only four pieces of information in our mind at one time[2] but can focus on only one of these.[3]

Keeping students focused

It generally appears that many students start becoming overloaded in about 15-20 minutes unless the lesson is very interesting.[4] It is easier to maintain focused attention when the person is physically and emotionally involved. Whole body movement can be incorporated into lessons. Ideally, students would be up and moving to a different location, engaging in a different sort of mentally-challenging task, so overloaded neural networks are given a chance to recover. Better still is an activity that can generate an accelerated heart and respiratory rate. That changes the brain's chemistry and prepares the body to take in new information for a longer period of time.[5]

Using movement to engage the attention system and promote the brain's readiness to learn requires re-thinking how we design lessons. With young children, creating a pause in the lesson for some game-playing is fun for children and feels natural.

As children move towards adolescence, they frequently reject the contrived body movement games. They remark that such movement is embarrassing, so we need to investigate how significant movement can be incorporated without it becoming a liability to the learning. Possibilities include game-playing, pantomimes, and paired students walking and talking about an assigned topic. As activities raise the respiratory and heart rate, students' levels of attention change rapidly.

A natural reaction by many teachers is that the 'play' wastes valuable time. However, when you realize the necessity of re-teaching because students missed key information due to being bored, zoned out, or overloaded, it soon becomes apparent that short refreshing activities actually allow the students to be more productive and increases efficient use of instructional time.

Paying attention to ADHD

ADHD students face a different challenge in controlling and maintaining their attention. Approximately 5-8% of both boys and girls have ADHD,[6] although it is frequently missed in girls because they express it differently.[7] The frontal lobes of the brain, whose executive functions help regulate attention, are typically underactive.[8] Their brain seeks stimulation and many classrooms don't provide enough of it, hence their minds wander, or their brains direct their bodies to move, tap, squirm, or fidget. Since the brain is seeking stimulation, their spontaneous, unregulated movements appear to be attempts by the brain to self-medicate and get the stimulation it needs.

One of the worst directives we can give the student is to tell them to: "Stop moving, be quiet and pay attention!" Brain scans have revealed that even more of the brain's prefrontal lobe goes 'off-line' when students try to be quiet and concentrate.[9] When teachers stop them moving, aiming to force concentration, the brain becomes considerably less functional, making it more likely that the student won't learn. The student brain needs stimulation.

Where possible, strategically-timed physical activities help. Obviously educators can't provide continuous activity, but some needs can be addressed unobtrusively.

For example, students who cannot sit still, and need movement, can be seated on a large physical education ball as they work on assignments. The extra effort to remain balanced on the ball provides the extra stimulus the brain needs, allowing them to stay more focused on the lesson. One strategy I have used is to empower the students with a rudimentary knowledge of how their brain works. Thus, when a student is directed to stand at a desk or even on one foot and take notes they realize the directive is not a punishment but a way of helping them, and they learn to stimulate themselves when they need to.

The role of emotional connections

My friend and colleague, Bob Greenleaf, author of *Creating and Changing Mindsets*,[10] suggests: 'Make the emotional connection first, then worry about the lesson.' Emotional processing by the student has a profound impact on how the student learns and should not be underestimated. Even minor comments uttered in passing may be harbored by the student for years and may influence their actions.

All of our lessons are processed and evaluated to some extent by their emotional impact, including the unintentional actions of the teacher, and the content of the lesson itself. By understanding how emotional processing works, educators can more directly design and control the emotional impact of a lesson. In turn, the lesson's emotional significance to the student can make a lasting memory. Most of us can recall a few powerfully emotional events that gave shape to our lives. Carefully crafted lessons can have such power. If an emotional connection is created early in the lesson, before the multitude of details, the learning potential has just jumped.

Impact of emotional salience on attention and motivation

Within milliseconds of detecting patterns, newly detected information is processed through one of two pathways, an urgent direct path, or a slower frontal cortex pathway. In either case, patterns are processed through a structure called the amygdala, which acts somewhat like an emotional filter. The information is first rapidly and crudely examined for its personal significance, asking 'is this a threat to me or not?'[11] If not, it generally is not given much, if any, direct attention. A slower, second network in the prefrontal lobes of the brain processes the information more thoroughly so it may be given more careful attention.

Emotionally-charged information usually captures our attention and is better remembered than unemotional, or not personally significant, information.[12] The level of personal or emotional significance is called *salience*.

Much traditional teaching has little salience to the students. Consequently it is almost immediately ignored by the student's brain without them even being aware of it. It is unconsciously being dumped, creating a huge dilemma for educators. We can make lessons very emotionally significant by creating high stress. For example, we might employ high-stakes testing for failing students. It is well established in research that too much stress makes for poor learning;[13] moreover it is ethically and morally improper.

As much instructional content can lack salience for many students, how can we increase it, especially when what is important to one student may be utterly boring to the next? It is still an art, something that seems to distinguish the gifted teacher. The brain does not work by a mechanistic blueprint plan.

A salient atmosphere

Educators can start by directly facilitating the creation of a positive and emotionally charged lesson with their own body language. This is accomplished not by the words we say but by the tone of voice we use and the enthusiasm we display. The pattern recognition of excitement serves to focus our attention, and prepares the brain emotionally for information that is probably not a threat, but novel and interesting.

Salient caring

If students can relate the task to their own life experiences, the salience increases still more. They care about the outcome.

First, the educator should clearly show that they *genuinely* care about the student as a person. If not, the student will soon detect it. The response to both the teacher and lesson will change for a number of students, simply because the teacher really cares about them. In turn, many students will mirror caring about the teacher and start wanting to please them on some level.[14] Part of this response seems to involve mirror neurons which contribute to communication and the power of modeling.

Second, and more difficult to accomplish, is to get to know the student on a personal level, including knowing about their life outside of school. This new knowledge can become especially powerful. It allows the teacher to better address when it is appropriate to change an assignment and requirements, much like coaching an athlete. For example, perhaps the student has a special interest to incorporate, or has been up all night, so their performance will be suboptimal the next day from stress and sleep deprivation.[15]

A third way to start connecting emotionally with students occurs with communication. This will vary with cultural norms. When conversing *with* the student, or perhaps when giving directions, be at eye level or lower. This sends an immediate, non-verbal message that you're not a threat, but trying to communicate with the student. Whether *eye contact* is appropriate depends upon the culture. In some cultures eye contact is generally not acceptable and may be considered an affront.

The message is, 'know your culture', because cultural norms will impact on how to connect emotionally with the student. Communication goes in both directions, *with* the student, not *to* the student. If communication is truly opened, there is a better chance the student will start thinking rather than just responding. Then the student can be involved at a much deeper level, with greater salience adding to better learning.

Children's frontal lobes aren't finished

Among the last areas of the brain to finish developing are in the very front of the brain, the prefrontal lobes that rest above our eyes, which don't mature until between 21 and 24 years.[16] The prefrontal region has major executive functions in decision-making. It processes much of our impulsivity or inhibition control, emotional control, focused attention in working memory, logic and reasoning. That's why the inhibition controls of children and young adults are incompletely grown.[17] Youth can certainly learn superb study skills, but even many of the brightest students will not initiate use of those skills without some direction being given. Their brains' 'start and stop' networks that function as control switches do have the neural wiring in place, but the insulation that is provided by myelin is not complete, leading to faulty control.

Both parents and teachers commonly intone sternly: "Didn't you think of the consequences of that action!" Unfortunately, adolescents consider consequences rather infrequently. The *normal* process at this stage of development is *not* to think fully about the consequences. Unfortunately the admonition is largely inappropriate and unrealistic because of brain development until more of their inhibitory controls become functional. *We* have to be their frontal lobe. The more we understand the developmental basis, the more we can have developmentally appropriate expectations for our students.

Memory, learning and plasticity

Learning is arguably all about the formation of retrievable memories, which includes the knowledge, processes, habits, skills, attitudes, and even biases that make up perceptions by which we learn to view or analyze something. For educational purposes, the majority of what we call learning is memory that can be retrieved upon demand and the perceptions that have been developed through experiences. One of the most basic properties of the brain is its plasticity, the ability to change.

The changes occur in the strengths of the synaptic connections. If it weren't for plasticity, and changing those synaptic connections, then we couldn't lay down new memories and learn. Likewise, if strengths of the connections didn't weaken, another feature of the brain's plasticity, we wouldn't forget either. Since learning and memory are inextricably intertwined, it is essential that we understand the characteristics of memory and how to make memories that are more easily retrieved.

Use it or lose it: neural and synaptic pruning

One of the most important demonstrations of plasticity in learning is the principle of *use it or lose it*. We are born with an overabundance of neurons and synaptic connections between them, and by late adolescence two major rounds of synaptic pruning have occurred. Synaptic pruning eliminates connections that are infrequently used while stronger connections are kept and strengthened.

In pruning, synaptic connections that *are* used are maintained and create more connections to other neurons. This builds up a cognitive reserve, something like a bank account of information and memories. In late adulthood, we can draw upon that cognitive reserve of synaptic connections to stay functioning and maintain some independence.

If, however, a person has taken the least challenging way all their life, and did not 'use it', they banked less cognitive reserve. This has potentially huge consequences for both the individual and society, since their brain span won't match their lifespan. Their brain stops being sufficiently functional years before their body quits. We either use the brain, increasing our brain span, or lose cognitive function.

Types of memory

Memory is sorted into three forms, depending upon how long it lasts.

Sensory memory
Sensory memory is the first stage through which information passes and is the most brief, lasting only tenths of a second. For example the still image of a movie frame remains in sensory memory long enough for the brain to blend it into the next frame, creating the illusion of motion that we see in the cinema.

Working memory
The next stage that information passes through on its way to becoming learned is working memory (WM), lasting from about one second to around a minute before it fades. Working memory is whatever one is currently thinking about or attending to at this moment, and appears to be a blend of the newest incoming information and information retrieved from long-term memory.[18]

However, at any given moment the amount of information being attended to is relatively small. WM's limited capacity to attend to information continuously generates problems. The brain always has the ability to store more memory. Unlike a computer, it doesn't fill up.

However, WM is rapidly overloaded if information comes in too fast. Imagine a single small door that opens into a huge auditorium. Everything that enters that final hall must pass through the door. If too many people try to squeeze through all at once, a jam up occurs. The information that the brain can't comprehend, because it arrives too fast, is usually lost, in the same way that people who can't squeeze through the door may give up and leave.

Working memory and learning
For information to be learned it must first get into WM and be actively processed there. Otherwise it is extremely unlikely that it will get through the door to be stored in the more permanent long-term memory. If the WM is so easily

overwhelmed or overloaded, what information will make it into the memory, what happens to the other information? And most importantly, what can we do about it?

To demonstrate some of the limits, we'll conduct a brief thought experiment right here, in text. Follow the directions precisely and no cheating! You'll need a piece of paper and something to write with. In the next couple of sentences follow along with your finger as you read. The moment you become aware that you cannot recall verbatim every single word, stop reading.

Working memory reading experiment

A major problem with working memory is the issue of capacity, how much a person can actually hold in their mind at a given moment, because if that capacity can somehow be increased, we can solve more complex problems faster. Are there such limits to capacity, and are there strategies to increase the capacity? We'll explore that shortly.

Now cover the paragraph above and without peeking, try to write down the sentences with no errors. How far did you get? A typical educator with a college degree probably wouldn't make it to the end of the first sentence while still able to recall the information verbatim. In fact, very few people are able to recall an entire sentence. The brain was easily overwhelmed and only the gist of the message was retained; the rest was dumped from the mind. A similar problem occurs with the spoken word. Within just one or two sentences the brain has started to overload and shed details, leaving only the gist. Clearly in teaching we want the students to be able to retain and retrieve not only the gist, but often critical details and inferred relationships that help explain the gist.

'Chunking' information to keep the mind/brain systems on task

As we've just experienced in the above experiment, information that is not attended to, or being actively thought about, is rapidly lost. WM works something like a desktop with a limited capacity.[19] The desktop rapidly becomes covered as newer information arrives in a constant stream, making space for itself by shoving out the slightly older information. Unless the older information, now well-aged at perhaps 30-45 seconds, is again actively used in thought, it promptly fades and is lost.

If the incoming information is organized by some trait, it can be 'chunked'.[20] In our desktop analogy, that would mean the new information doesn't come in a piece at a time and rapidly covers the desk, but as a large stack of information that occupies a much smaller area. As described in the section on attention, it appears that we can usually only thoroughly focus our attention and think about one item. Other items of attention can be juggled but, for most people, those items are not really focused upon.[21] But when ideas are combined properly, the mind can focus on this one 'chunk'.

Brain breaks

Brain breaks are a relatively simple way of substantially reducing the overloading of WM and subsequent loss of information. This is an easy, practical classroom procedure where the teacher periodically pauses after about four to seven significant pieces of information, or stops at the very least about every 15-20 minutes, and conducts a short, rapid review.

The brain break review may take several forms, such as a short verbal or written quiz with about three to four questions. For example, describe two things that were just discussed, list three things that were just presented, and then have students get up and move to other desks in order to look at those student's lists and find one different from their own list (which also brings in movement). The brain break fires the new neural networks again, moving them a little closer to a more permanent memory. The new neural networks are fragile and not yet well-established, but the brain breaks begin to establish a more stable and retrievable memory.

When students are working on a task they tend to shift their attention away from listening. If instructions or other information must be given, have the students stop and redirect their attention so it is completely on the teacher. They cannot work on their task and listen to instructions equally well. This is an example of divided attention and demonstrates how quickly their WM is overloaded if they attempt both.

Lasting and useful memory

Some educators believe that: 'Waiting on the student will waste even more time and they've so much to learn!' In the long run, it is more efficient to go slower so they learn more, than to re-teach the missed portions of every lesson. Another issue is whether the goal is to have students learn some material deeply, or learn a lot of material shallowly. There is an emerging trend to focus more on a student's ability to understand deeply and develop the skills in order to apply appropriately key principles to new problems and leave the multitude of details for studies beyond the introductory courses.

The PYP has chosen to inquire into a limited number of units in depth, to provide for this deep learning. This is quite different from the traditional style that a university professor described as "...the fire hose approach, where we simply turn on a flood of information and hope the students are able to take a few drinks without drowning". M. Lyford (personal communication, March, 2008).

The learning process of building a retrievable memory is not a linear process where a magical number of repetitions will create the memory the students need. It is a highly dynamic and complex weave, building up connected neural networks to finally establish long-term memory. Indeed, there are examples of when students learned with a single lesson when the material had sufficient salience and the student brought a highly focused attention system to the task. And there can be an opposite situation where literally hundreds of repetitions produced no lasting memory. Sheer repetition for a subject doesn't necessarily produce excellent recall if it lacks significant salience.

What is long-term memory?

Memory generally appears to be distributed across the thin cortex that comprises the brain's surface. As we observed in WM, long-term memory is called upon to help process and interpret the latest information. The boundary between WM and long-term memory (LTM) is not distinct, but there are major properties that affect educational performance every day.

Much of what constitutes LTM memory is processed through, and temporarily stored in, the hippocampus, a structure found deep in the brain. Later the bits and pieces of the memory are moved to various areas of the cortex, where the bulk of LTM appears to be stored. The cortex is roughly 3-5mm thick and achieves part of its great storage capacity through the deep folds that characterize the brain. This allows more cortex to be crammed into an already confined space.

Memories for many concepts and ideas appear to be broken up and scattered throughout the cortex, although specific information is sometimes in a lone location (more on that later). When new information arrives, the strength of the connection is changed.[22] The stronger the connection, the easier to recall. The distribution of the information and the different strengths or weaknesses of the connections affect much of a student's educational performance. To see how this occurs we need to examine the properties of LTM more closely.

Explicit, episodic and implicit LTM

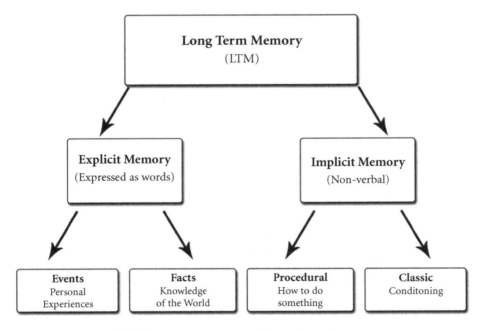

Figure 1. Basic model of long-term memory forms that educators encounter.

While there are many properties to memory, only a few forms can be directly manipulated to change a student's performance. Most traditional lessons primarily rely upon a form of memory for knowledge of facts called *explicit* memory. Because there is often little personal link with this knowledge such memories are more difficult to recall.

To a lesser extent *episodic* memories, a form of explicit memory for personally experienced events, can provide particularly powerful access to memory because they were experienced by the student, and hence have salience. However, traditional lesson designs commonly overlook memories for personal actions or procedures that cannot be expressed in words, but are observed by demonstration or performance. Memories of this form are called *implicit* memories (see Figure 1). They can be one of the most powerful forms of memory that, by their very nature, have high salience and are more easily recalled.

Using implicit memories

Many lessons rely heavily on explicit memory, which students often cannot retrieve. However, when lessons that are loaded with facts and knowledge are combined with implicit non-verbal procedures, robust memories can be formed and retrieved for long periods of time after the lesson.

To summarize, a very robust memory can result when students repeatedly explain and simultaneously model what they are doing, creating multiple neural networks of different memory types. The movement involved in their modeling or physical performance also allows immediate feedback on accuracy, further increasing salience for the activity.

Memory can be fickle, as so many of us have personally experienced. Sometimes learning requires only a single occurrence because it holds such great significance for the learner. Let me illustrate. Each of the following events is a form of explicit memory but with differences in salience for the reader.

Can you recall your first algebra test, or Diana, Princess of Wales' death? Where were you when the World Trade Center Twin-Towers collapsed; the first time you made love? The greater the personal significance, the easier it is to recall. In terms of our survival, recalling such events would be clearly advantageous and appears to be an evolutionary adaptation. Little effort or studying is necessary because of the emotional significance. Additionally, many of these memories carry a large amount of detail with them, all without studying.

Imagine for a moment if students were able to have lessons of great personal significance but without the negative threat. Retrieval from memory would be considerably easier. We can create linkages between a given lesson and student by facilitating their search for patterns, and having the students physically involved, especially where they have a personal interest in the outcome, to help maintain their attention and reduce overload. These are things the educator can do to create a better memory.

Multiple modes of learning

A key strength of the PYP's transdisciplinary approach is to allow students to explore a complex area using different subjects and 'modes of learning'.

Instead of using a single instructional modality, transdisciplinary learning allows students to use multiple modalities of learning and memory within a single lesson. For example, a lesson might start with direct teacher explanation, followed by students elaborating on lesson topics using personal drawings, and finally by students describing events related to the topic that they have experienced. This lesson uses explicit forms of semantic and episodic memory as well as some procedural memory, all building multiple, but different networks to the same concept.

Each modality of instruction networked to the same topic becomes important in a later retrieval. Having multiple networks or pathways to the same information increases the likelihood of retrieving the desired information. In contrast, when a student learns by one form, the retrieval of a memory is easily disrupted. For example, a student can learn large volumes of content by using a mnemonic, where each memorized letter represents some word. However, access to the information is easily lost if the student forgets the mnemonic because of reliance on a single memory pathway. By creating multiple pathways using different modes of instruction or differentiated instruction, the memory is more likely to be retrieved when needed.

High levels of stress can also interfere with memory, while slight stress can keep the students more alert. For example, under stressful test conditions, or while speaking in front of a large group of people, the memory for a particular piece of information may be temporarily blocked. Later, when the person is no longer in the stressful situation, the name or piece of information suddenly pops into mind. The connection has been re-established, albeit a bit late. It follows that if the high stress that is perceived by the student can be reduced, and if they are able to relax, such blockages are less likely.

Earlier, I mentioned that memory for a concept tends to be broken up and spread throughout the cortex. When the memory network is accessed we don't connect to the entire network for that memory, but to a portion of it. As a result we never have exactly the same thought twice. Multiple assessments, using different modalities, are necessary to overcome the limited access to the memory of a concept at any particular time, so that we get a clearer idea of what is in the student's brain.

This aspect is well known to emergency workers, police investigators and the military. They use multiple debriefings of personnel to pick up on important information that was missed earlier. A single assessment gives only a poor snapshot of what is in the brain and may miss large portions of what a student knows. This becomes evident when the topics are discussed with the student in a non-test environment.

Mirror neurons

There is a key neurological reason why modeling can contribute powerfully in building a memory, and it involves mirror neurons. They are specialized neurons that are involved in many learning processes. As the name suggests, these neurons help a person to mirror (model or imitate) the actions of others, even if we don't move, but merely think about or watch another person. If we watch a person pick up a cup of tea, the same areas in our brain that are needed to pick up a cup are also activated, except we aren't moving. If we watch a bad crash in the Tour de France we wince, as if we feel the pain. The same areas of the brain are involved. The neurons allow a person to emphasize, to 'feel' what the other person is experiencing.

Mirror neurons' impact on learning

Mirror neurons have a key role because of their ability to allow us mentally to mimic and activate the same areas in our brain, that were used in the person we are watching. The result is we can change our performance by simply watching or thinking about someone else's actions. As Dijksterhuis observed, 'Relevant research has shown by now that imitation can make us slow, fast, smart, stupid, good at math, bad at math, helpful, rude, polite, long-winded, hostile, aggressive...'[23]

It is far more complex than monkey see, monkey do.[24] But it does suggest why we might think at a higher level when we are around scholars from Harvard or Cambridge, than say when we are with our beer drinking friends at a football match! Mirror neurons, as they are closely related to uncontrolled biological automaticity, also appear to be involved with the development of addictions and relapses, impulse buying, and media violence, especially violent video games.[25] With the data pouring in from studies on media violence and subsequent imitative violent acts, the importance of mirror neurons becomes even more evident since this also potentially impacts our cherished notions of free-will, and of why some actions are clearly not rational.[26]

Mirror neurons may also be involved in a lack of access to a memory or the forgetting of some information, as shown by sparse coding and the so-called 'Jennifer Aniston cell'.[27] It was found that some types of information, in this case about the movie star Jennifer Aniston, appear to reside entirely in a single cell (even though it may have a few thousand connections through the dendrites to other cells). Researchers are not certain exactly how this works because we still don't know precisely how a memory is built from the cell's chemistry.

If that cell was to die, or there was a lesion (injury) to the cell and access to it was broken, it is presumed that all information related to that topic would also be lost since it appears to reside in no other location. It seems that information may be in a single or a few related cells. The theory of sparse coding suggests that only a few neurons are activated for a particular concept, rather than just one.[28] If that applies to educational topics, it might suggest, at least in part, why students sometimes seem to completely lose a piece of information. The many roles of mirror neurons are still not clear, but our understanding of them continues to grow, bringing potential for better teaching in the future.

Conclusions

Now that neuroeducation is providing key insights into how we learn, there are many practical ways that educators can change their practice so that our students learn better. We can help our students see patterns by guiding them with questions and helping them to look more critically at information. We appreciate the importance of students by connecting personally to their learning, and by teachers building emotional bridges with the students. We need to be aware of how easily their attention and working memory system is overwhelmed, and that they really only focus on one task at time, and learn it in depth.

After a concept is established, students should go further and build a wider variety of connections using their different learning modalities. They should revisit and reinforce the concepts and the connections to those concepts. If they don't use it, they will rapidly lose it.

Both non-ADHD and ADHD students can be supported by addressing their brain's need for the vigorous movement that helps to keep them on task. All students need brain breaks to avoid overloading and to permit the students to quickly review and reinforce what they just did. Remember they are children and their brains are still growing; they don't have full control over their judgment or impulses, and they rarely think about consequences.

A final point is that *our* brains are still learning too, and *we must also use it or lose it*. Any new skills or techniques that we have acquired will need to be reinforced on a frequent basis. Neuroeducation is a powerful tool that provides direction for both student and teacher as learners throughout their lives.

References

1. Cherry, E.C. (1953): Some experiments on the recognition of speech, with one and two ears, in *Journal of the Acoustic Society of America*, 25, pp975-979.

2. Oberauer, K. (2002): Access to information in working memory: Exploring the focus of attention, in *Journal of Experimental Psychology: Learning, Memory, and Cognition*, 28, pp411-421.

3. Cowan, N. (2001): The magical number 4 in short-term memory: A reconsideration of mental storage capacity, in *Behavioral and Brain Sciences*, 24, pp87-185.

4. Schenck, J. (2003): *Learning, teaching, and the brain. A practical guide for educators.* Thermopolis.WY: Knowa Publishing.

5. Ratey, J. (2008): *Spark, the revolutionary new science of exercise and the brain.* NY: Little, Brown and Company.

6. Barkley, R. (1998): *Attention Deficit Hyperactivity Disorder, a handbook for diagnosis and treatment.* NY: Guilford Press. 2nd Edition.

7. Nadeau, K., Littman, E., and Quinn, P. (1999): *Understanding girls with ADHD*. Washington D.C: Advantage Books.

8. Seig, K.G., Gaffney, G.R., Preston, D.F., and Hellings, J.A. (1995): SPECT brain imaging abnormalities in attention deficit hyperactivity disorder, in *Clinical Nuclear Medicine*, 20, pp55-60.

9. Zametkin, A.J., Nordahl, T.E., Gross, M., King, A.C., Semple, W.E., Rumsey, J., Hamburger, S., and Cohen, R. M. (1990): Cerebral glucose metabolism in adults with hyperactivity of childhood onset, in the *New England Journal of Medicine*, 323, pp1361-1366.

10. Greenleaf, R.K. (2005): *Creating and Changing Mindsets, Movies of The Mind: strategies for long-term impact upon change and the Acts of Achievement, Motivation and Relationship Building.* Greenleaf Learning, Maine. (www.greenleaflearning.com)

11. LeDoux, J. (1996): *The Emotional brain: The mysterious underpinnings of emotional life*. NY: Simon & Schuster.

12. Marx, B., Marshall, P., and Castro, F. (2008): The moderating effects of stimulus valence and arousal on memory suppression, in *Emotion*, 8(2), pp199-207.

13. Schooler, J., and Eich, E. (2000): Memory for emotional events, in Tulving, E., and Craik, F.I.M. (Eds): *The Oxford handbook of memory*, pp379-392.

14. Iacoboni, M. (2008): *Mirroring people*. NY: Farrar, Straus and Giroux.

15. Miller, N., Shattuck, L., Matsangas, P., and Dyche, J. (2008): Sleep and academic performance in U.S. military training and education programs, in *Mind, Brain, and Education* (2)1, pp29-33.

16. Fischer, K., and Rose, L. (2001): Webs of skill: How students learn, in *Educational Leadership*, pp6-12.

17. Fischer, K., and Rose, S. (1998): Growth Cycles of brain and mind, in *Educational Leadership*, 56(3), pp56-60.

18. Cowan, N. (2005): *Working Memory Capacity*. NY: Psychological Press.

19. Baddeley, A. (1990): *Human Memory: theory and practice*. Boston. Allyn and Bacon. 1st Edition.

20. Miller, G. (1956): The magical number seven, plus or minus two: Some limits on our capacity for processing information, in *Psychological Review*, 63, pp81-97.

21. Cowan, N. (2005): *Working Memory Capacity*. NY: Psychological Press.

22. Freeman, W. (2001): *How brains make up their minds*. NY: Columbia University Press.

23. Dijksterhuis, A., (2005): Why we are social animals: The high road to imitation as a social glue, in Hurley, S., and Chater, N. (Eds): *Perspectives on Imitation*, 2, pp207-20.

24. Iacoboni, M., (2008): *Mirroring people*. NY: Farrar, Straus and Giroux.

25. Anderson, C., Gentile, D., and Buckley, K. (2007): *Violent video game effects on children and adolescents: theory, research, and public policy*. NY: Oxford University Press.

26. Hurley, S. (2004): Imitation, media violence, and freedom of speech, in *Philosophical Studies*, 117, pp165-218.

27. Quiroga, R., Reddy, L., Kreiman, G., *et al.* (2005): Invariant visual representations by single neurons in the human brain, in *Nature*, 435, pp1102-07.

28. Gallese, V., Fadiga, L., Fogassi, L., *et al.*, (1996): Action Recognition in the Premotor Cortex, in *Brain*, 119(2), pp593-609.

Chapter 10

The pre-primary schools of Reggio Emilia

Pam Oken-Wright

Do nothing without joy.
Loris Malaguzzi

Reggio Emilia is a city of about 142,000 people in the region of Emilia Romagna in northern Italy. It is the birthplace of the Italian flag, the origin of the wonderful Parmigiano Reggiano cheese we import, and the home of a world-class system of public pre-primary schools. The more than 30 infant-toddler centers and preschools in Reggio Emilia have garnered worldwide attention for the high level of work done by children and teachers, for extraordinarily beautiful school environments, and for the tremendous community support the schools enjoy.

Many educators in the United States first learned of the schools of Reggio Emilia from a *Newsweek* article published in 1991, in which the pre-primary schools of Reggio Emilia were acclaimed as the world's best in early childhood education.[1] In 1998, Howard Gardner described the schools of Reggio Emilia as:

> 'a collection of schools for young children in which each child's intellectual, emotional, social, and moral potentials are carefully cultivated and guided. The principal educational vehicle involves youngsters in long-term engrossing projects, which are carried out in a beautiful, healthy, love-filled setting... Nowhere else in the world is there such a seamless and symbiotic relationship between a school's progressive philosophy and its practices.'[2]

A brief history of the pre-primary schools of Reggio Emilia

At the conclusion of World War II and the end of the Fascist dictatorship in Italy, a group of determined parents in Reggio Emilia began to build, with their own hands, a school for their young children. That is where Loris Malaguzzi, the 'guiding genius' of the Reggio philosophy,[3] found them and where a collaboration between educators and parents began and endures to this day.

In the 1950s and 1960s, Reggio teachers, led by Malaguzzi, embraced a goal of innovation in education, inspired by the thinking of John Dewey, Jean Piaget, and Lev Vygotsky. The desire to put current learning theory into practice has endured throughout the history of the pre-primary schools in Reggio Emilia, including the theories of Jerome Bruner, Howard Gardner, and others. In the 1960s, the pre-primary schools of Reggio Emilia became municipally supported.

A quick look at the schools of Reggio Emilia

The preschools and infant-toddler centers of Reggio Emilia offer full-day programs to children from all socioeconomic backgrounds; children with disabilities, referred to as children with special rights in Reggio Emilia, have priority in placement. The schools do not have directors; the teachers share the responsibilities of running the schools. Two teachers work as equal collaborators in each classroom, supported by a pedagogical coordinator (*pedagogista*), who may travel between two or more schools, and a studio teacher (*atelierista*). Teachers and children stay together for three-year cycles: three in the infant-toddler centers (ages 0 to three) and another three in the preschools (ages three to six).

The schools, each with its own identity, are 'amiable' places[4] that emanate 'welcome' to children and parents. Light and transparency, living plants, natural materials, and peaceful colors lend the spaces a serene, inviting atmosphere. Documentation panels line the walls. These exquisite displays, with photographs of children working, accompanied by text of teachers' and children's thinking about the experience, make the teaching and learning in the school visible to all who enter.

Children's work in many media, often accompanied by their reflection or by that of their teachers, is everywhere. The children in the Reggio schools are engaged, self-directed, and collaborative. They consider themselves, and are considered by others, to be agents of important work. In every preschool and infant-toddler center I visited in Reggio Emilia, the teachers' beliefs about children, teaching, and learning were clearly apparent in their interaction with the children and in the environment. Those beliefs form the basis for a set of principles that inform all practice in the Reggio schools.

Guiding principles of the Reggio Emilia philosophy

As far as I know, there is no 'definitive' list of Reggio principles. Indeed, a study of the literature reveals many variations, often including the same ideas but with slightly different organization. In fact, the Reggio Emilia philosophy is organic, with each 'principle' weaving in and out of the others; thus it defies the very categorization that might help us understand it better. So, as you read this set of principles, or similar ones, notice how each affects the other; imagine them as threads woven into whole cloth, rather than a list of distinct and separate ideas.

The image of the child

Every child is considered competent, resourceful, full of potential, in search of relationship with others and ideas, and an active agent in his or her own learning from birth. Teachers' interactions with children are, therefore, highly respectful of the children themselves, of their experiences and culture, and of their work. Teachers also trust that, given a chance, children will gravitate toward that which challenges them and is worth knowing.

The school environment

Most who enter an infant-toddler center or preschool in Reggio Emilia for the first time, are struck by both the beauty of the school and the way that the children's presence is apparent in the space, whether the children are physically there or not. Visible throughout the building are images of the children and their work, as well as evidence of children's families, culture, and experiences.

The educators of Reggio Emilia refer to the environment as a 'third teacher'. They recognize that a school environment can invite children to work collaboratively or alone. It can invite self-sufficiency and interdependence or dependence on adults. It can invite harmony or discord. It can exhaust or energize. The teachers of Reggio Emilia set up school environments to foster collaboration, self-sufficiency, harmony, joy, and energy. They prepare the environment carefully and intentionally to call the children to intellectual pursuit through what they call 'provocations'. A provocation might be a question or challenge, or it might be a new, intriguing object or a change in the environment, offered to children as an invitation to discovery, investigation, and joy.

Symbolic representation

Constructivist educators know that knowledge cannot be transmitted. Rather, the learner acts on information in some way to construct knowledge. Representing one's ideas is vital to this process. When we talk through an idea or take notes in class or write a paper we are representing the ideas presented as information. Young children have powerful ideas – ideas so expansive and elusive that they often cannot represent them to their satisfaction with verbal language alone. But they can make their most profound ideas visible through drawing, painting, sculpting, constructing, moving, making music, and other graphic and temporal media. In Reggio Emilia, educators refer to all the ways in which children can represent their ideas as 'the hundred languages of children'.

They make multiple media available to the children from a very early age – many kinds of pens and paints, potter's clay, materials for collage and construction, wire for sculpting, and looms for weaving, for example. Teachers support the children's learning about what the media can do and what the media lets the children do, so that the children have many ways to make their ideas visible.

Through representation in all these media, the children are able to delve more deeply into topics that interest them, and they also learn to translate their ideas from one medium to another. For example, a child might paint a picture of a tree, draw it, sculpt it in three dimensions, and engage in conversation with others about its multiple attributes to arrive at an understanding of 'tree' that is satisfying to him or her.

All Reggio teachers work to support children's learning through representation. Small groups of children also work in the *atelier* with a studio teacher (*atelierista*) to explore and learn about media, to work on collaborative projects, and to represent their ideas through multiple media. In addition, each classroom has a mini-*atelier*, in which small groups of children can work on ongoing projects in the context of their classroom.

Collaboration

Collaboration is 'the backbone of the system' in Reggio Emilia.[5] It is, to a large degree, what makes the remarkable results of the Reggio schools possible. Each classroom has two teachers who work as equals, collaborating to plan, facilitate, document, and research. Children collaborate with each other toward shared goals in play and project work. Teachers collaborate with children in the course of investigation. Children may bring an idea to teachers, or teachers may bring one to children, but, however an investigation begins, children and teachers work together to figure out what aspect of the idea speaks to the children and how they might develop a deeper understanding of the idea.

For those studying the Reggio philosophy this principle may be one of the most elusive, as learning is not directed by either children or teachers. Rather, children and teachers work together, constructing the experience of studying a topic as they go along, creating together the path the investigation will take.

Reggio teachers consider the education of the child to be a collaborative venture among teacher, child, parent, and community. Parents assume many roles in the collaborative process, including serving on advisory councils. Teachers and parents of children engaged in a particular project, may meet together to explore opportunities and possibilities for supporting the children's inquiry; they may meet together to create a surprise for the children or work together to enhance the school environment.

When they are in the school parents can read documentation of children's ongoing and recent experiences. The schools of Reggio Emilia enjoy a remarkable level of support from parents. Lilian Katz suggests that this support may be due to the high quality of experiences the schools offer to their children.[6]

Most of the project work in Reggio schools is done in small groups. According to recent research about the relationship between group learning and individual learning, children learn better with the perspectives of others than when alone. In addition, the individual contributes to the collective knowledge of the group, knowledge greater than any of the group's members could have constructed alone, and which they all share.[7] In a Reggio or Reggio-inspired classroom children seek each other out in order to collaborate in play, solve problems, and exchange ideas.

Teachers use many different strategies to support this rich exchange; for example, they may refer a child to another child who has solved a similar problem in the past, or who has expertise in a particular area (from tying shoes to writing); encourage children to invite collaboration; help children work together to solve problems while refraining from solving problems for children; and invite children to join small groups for project work. Even the way the environment is arranged encourages group work.

The teacher's roles

A teacher's role in Reggio Emilia is complex. There are no scope and sequence to follow; there are no manuals. Each investigation with children is new, negotiated from the beginning by teacher and children together.

As children work and play in an environment arranged with care to encourage collaborative, thoughtful endeavors, teachers observe and document. They are alert about when to step in to offer materials, techniques, or tools, whatever they think will support the children's work, without doing it for them. Observers in Reggio schools are sometimes surprised that teachers become as involved as they do in children's projects. The difference between enough and too much intervention seems to lie in teachers' ability to listen intuitively to the child and read the situation, rather than focusing on the adult's agenda. If a teacher intervenes with respect for the child's vision and with the intention of helping him accomplish what he is trying to do or take his idea a step further, the child's vision remains intact and he is inclined to continue toward his goal.

Teachers in Reggio Emilia listen with more than their ears. They value listening as a whole-mind, whole-heart endeavor. When they intervene in children's play and representation they do so with considerable intention, perhaps asking themselves, what are the children trying to do? Are they satisfied with the way it's going? Is there something I can do to help them pursue their goal according to their own vision? If so, what would be of most help without interrupting the flow of ideas?

The teachers also act as memory keepers for the children. To help them to carry an idea through to fruition, a teacher may hold the children's current ideas for them until the next time they can meet; then she may invite the children to reflect on those ideas further and consider the topic anew. The documentation a teacher creates can also be a 'memory keeper' for the children; children can peruse documentation of a shared experience, using it as a bookmark of sorts so that together they can revisit their work and proceed from there.

The Reggio teacher is a researcher of children and how they learn. She conducts her research through documentation, which involves not only gathering data and creating a history of the investigation at hand and the experiences she and the children have shared, but also interpreting that data to understand the children's thinking and learning as deeply as possible.

Documentation

Documentation is the visible trace of children's experiences, thinking, learning, and process and the teachers' interpretation of the meaning of those experiences. Teachers take notes and photographs of children's learning processes, collect the children's representations or images of them, tape-record children's conversation and thinking, and collect artifacts of project work. At the end of a project (investigation) they organize all the documentation data collected, add narrative (the story of what happened), and interpretation (their hypothesis of what it means), and they create beautiful and insightful displays.

The displays can take many forms, among them panels on walls, notebooks, books, videos, and the children's own artifacts. This documentation, visible everywhere one goes in the school, serves to inspire children to remember and revisit experiences, to inform parents and visitors of the process and meaning of a project as seen by teachers, and to support teachers' understanding of the meaning of the project.

The creation of documentation products is only one step in a much larger process of understanding children's learning and relationships, and it may come fairly late in the life of an investigation or project. Much important documentation goes on long before a wall panel is ever created. Teachers document daily; they are as likely to record one child's process while making a painting as they are to document the process of a major investigation. Years ago, inspired by a triptych with teachers' notes and illustrative drawings that were posted outside the classrooms in a Reggio Emilia preschool, I began to make daily logs in our junior kindergarten at St Catherine's School in Richmond, Virginia.

Each day, I compile documentation data into a log that reflects the experiences important to the group. Each log contains narrative, illustrative photographs of the children's process, children's work or images of it, transcripts of any important conversations, an occasional video clip, and, where appropriate, reflections about the meaning the children or I construct from the experience being documented. The daily log is published on a webpage, password protected and accessible to parents and other protagonists in the children's learning story. I also print out a copy and keep it in the classroom as reference for children, teachers, and parents. Periodically I review the daily logs, looking for patterns in children's thinking and interests and considering possibilities. I may use them to pull an entire investigation together to make a more permanent form of documentation.

It is this initial documentation that helps me to see the meaning of what happened on a particular day and consider next steps – whether to sit tight and observe a little longer, offer a new provocation, or take the children's ideas back to them for more conversation. We document, in part, in an effort to understand children's intent in their play, conversation, and representation.

What is it that the children are trying to understand, for example, by returning to the same idea in play over and over and over? It is with this question that teachers approach interpretation of documentation data, and with which they formulate hypotheses about children's understanding, interests, passions, confusions, and perspectives. Those hypotheses are guesses about what is important to the children at a particular point in time, and they inform teachers' decisions about provocations to offer or challenges to pose. In this way documentation shapes curriculum.

At its best, documentation makes children's learning visible in ways conventional assessment tools cannot. Documentation of children's group work in daily and long term display, and of their progress in multiple dimensions in individual portfolios, give a much more complete image of a child's learning and development than grades or test scores ever could. Documentation makes learning *and* teaching transparent. The reflective teacher learns about children, their learning, and his own teaching in the process of making documentation and in its periodic review.

For all these reasons, documentation is fundamental to the Reggio Emilia approach, for it serves all who are involved in the children's learning: children; teachers; parents; administrators; and often the community.

A dynamic curriculum

Curriculum is a poor word for the learning that goes on in the schools of Reggio Emilia. The Italians have called the particular way of flexible planning for learning that teachers do *progettazione*. George Forman and Brenda Fyfe have called it negotiated learning,[8] rather like negotiating a slalom or a winding road. John Nimmo and Elizabeth Jones referred to it as emergent curriculum.[9]

Instead of working from scope and sequence or a prepared curriculum document, teachers observe and document children's play, conversation, and representation; study the documentation to try to really 'hear' what the children are meaning; and plan 'next steps' accordingly. There is a marvelous flow to all of this, a sort of organic quality and a connectedness. The 'next step' in the study of a topic is not likely to come out of the blue from the children's perspective, because that next step is determined in response to what the children themselves just said and did.

This approach requires a rather different disposition toward time than we may traditionally have held. Deep understanding never comes in a hurry, and it never obeys a timetable. In Reggio Emilia, a project may last a day or a year. A teacher's goal is to help children maintain their enthusiasm and engagement in an investigation as long as they can.

Sustained investigation takes time, of course, but from it children learn not only more about a topic than they could in a conventional early childhood curricular 'unit'. They also learn how to collaborate to co-construct theory; how to pursue an idea that interests them; how to express their ideas and theories to others; how to consider the ideas of others in the light of their own theories and experiences; how to have cognitive conflict without emotional conflict; how to reason in more and more sophisticated ways; and how to set a goal and to develop a satisfaction bar for oneself in meeting that goal – all dispositions that in essence create the inclination to live the life of a learner.

In a Reggio classroom, time is the learner's friend and teacher. Young children have long periods of time in which to play and work during the day. Teachers try to limit the number of interruptions to this work. Work that is not finished to the child's satisfaction can be continued the next day.

Children's co-construction of theory

Children construct theories about how the world works all the time. Teachers in the Reggio schools encourage children to explore those theories together through conversation and representation. The following story is an example of co-construction of theory in the context of an investigation about snow, conducted by a class of five-year-olds in our junior kindergarten class at St Catherine's School in Richmond, Virginia.

After a particularly big snowstorm, the children were full of images, conversation, and emotion about their experiences within the snow-covered world. The teacher observed the children's interest and excitement and when they sat down together at morning meeting she asked: "Tell me about snow." The children were used to having conversations as a group in which they posed theories about questions that intrigued them, and they quickly began wondering about the source of the snow.

The teacher recorded and transcribed the conversation. She then studied the transcript looking for, and discovering that there were, patterns in the children's theories. Most held that the source of snow was magic, with either God or Santa Claus an agent of that magic. Later the teacher took those theories back to the children, inviting them to consider them a little more. Again she listened to the conversation for other understandings and ideas. For several weeks the children continued to think about snow, representing snowflakes in paint, clay, found objects, blocks, and so forth. They continued to wonder about the source of snow.

The teacher invited the children to draw their ideas about the source of snow and to articulate their theories several times over the course of the project. At one point, the children thought that if they were able to make snow themselves they would discover the source of the snow that falls from the sky. The teacher helped the children clarify their thinking and express their ideas to each other when necessary. She helped them gather the materials they needed and offered support to work through stumbling blocks as the children experimented, failed, and tried again. But she did not scoop up the idea herself and take it on. She respected the children's agenda regarding snow, worked hard to understand what they were really trying to do, and supported them in their efforts to come to an answer that satisfied them.

When the children's experiments did not make snow, the children regrouped and decided that they needed to refer to experts. The fifth-graders, they thought, would know how to make snow. With the teacher's help, they interviewed the older children. As it turned out, the fifth-graders' theories were not much more sophisticated than those of the young children. However, the five-year-olds' sustained work of figuring out how it snows, eventually led them to a theory that satisfied them: snow starts as a tiny speck of ice and, in six stages (inspired by the six sides of a snowflake?) develops arms, detail and size, until it is a snowflake.

As often happens when five-year-olds 'live' with a question long enough, their theories evolved from highly magical to increasingly plausible and, finally, to close to accurate. Had the teacher told the children from the beginning what she knew about the source of snow, the children would have transformed that information into theories that made sense to them (often no more accurate, and maybe less than they would have constructed on their own), but they also most likely would have stopped constructing theory about the question, once they perceived that they had been told 'the truth' by an adult.

So, that first bit of theory constructed from the teacher's information would have been as far as the investigation went. Perhaps even more significant was that in working together over time to figure out how it snows, the children learned how to engage in inquiry. Furthermore, when children have grappled with an idea long enough, working together to grow theories that satisfy them, any information about the topic that crosses their path seems to become instantly theirs. They remain open to inquiry about the question for a long time, setting a far more receptive stage for learning in the future.[10]

The Reggio Emilia approach and the Primary Years Programme

The educators of Reggio Emilia caution us not to interpret their experiences as a teaching method. The approach cannot be 'transported' or 'adopted'. But there is much to learn from the experiences and reflections of the educators in Reggio Emilia. The principles that guide practice in the Reggio schools offer us insight and inspiration. The reflection that makes teaching a dynamic, alive process (reflection informs practice, which inspires further reflection) might inspire us to reconsider our current assumptions, as might such a high level of representation and thinking from such very young children.

The Reggio Emilia approach is not a method but a philosophy and set of guiding principles. Reggio teachers must be comfortable with not knowing in advance the topics of study, the paths investigations will take, or the end points. They must embrace the role of group learning. They must expect children to be capable of profound thinking and remarkable symbolic representation. They must embrace collaboration with colleagues and with parents. They must also be willing to invest time – time *with* children, time *for* children (interpreting documentation or collaborating with colleagues, for example), and time for their own learning.

A deep understanding of the Reggio philosophy can take many years to develop. Like children constructing an understanding of how it snows, teachers in a school work together to construct a place where children and teachers learn with joy and passion, in relationship and with mutual respect, reflective of their particular culture and context.

Discovering the principles of the Reggio Emilia philosophy has led many a constructivist teacher to a deeper translation of what it means to lead learning. They may find inspiration in the power of documentation, or a new vision for the environment, or a new set of parameters for inquiry-based learning. When I first encountered the Reggio Emilia approach I was a strong believer in constructivist teaching. Inquiry was at the core of the children's and my work. I had just begun to investigate the role of teacher mediation in work with children. Studying Reggio principles gave me the tools I needed to go a step deeper in my teaching. Documentation, small group work, and teacher research were my incomplete, if not entirely missing, pieces. Finding those missing pieces can make teaching and learning with children more satisfying for all.

Primary Years Programme teachers may see congruencies between the philosophy that informs their teaching and that of Reggio Emilia. For example, both are dedicated to supporting high-level thinking in children at all ages. Both view collaboration among children as a vital part of the inquiry process. Both value inquiry as central to the learning process.

You may notice differences as well. Inquiry in Reggio schools is not bounded by set units. Inquiry is likely to be followed by more inquiry. In other words, children investigate an idea, and rather than following that investigation with 'answers' teachers encourage children to revisit their hypotheses and theories. They may challenge the children's thinking or offer a new provocation to introduce information that challenges the children's theories.

Teachers recognize the value in sustained investigation; they understand that, generally, the longer children engage in meaningful investigation of an idea the deeper their understanding of the topic grows. And so they encourage children to sustain engagement in collaborative investigation of a topic as long as it proves worthwhile, making investigations of indefinite length. Until it is finished, teachers and learners do not know when or how an investigation will end. The result is that often children's learning is far deeper than that which teachers may have planned.

Notes

This chapter is adapted from Pam Oken-Wright, The Preprimary Schools of Reggio Emilia, in *Choosing The Right Educational Path For Your Child: What Are The Options?* Shields-West, E., and Carreira, P. (eds). (Rowman & Littlefield Education, 2008). It is reprinted here with permission.

The author thanks Lella Gandini and Judy Kaminsky for their advice and encouragement.

Information about current venues for 'The Hundred Languages of Children' exhibits is available on the website of the North American Reggio Emilia Association (NAREA): www.reggioalliance.org/narea/exhibit.php.

Further Reading

Cadwell, L. (1997): *Bringing Reggio Emilia Home.* New York: Teachers College Press.

Reggio Children, (1996): *The Catalogue of the Exhibit: The Hundred Languages of Children.* Reggio Emilia, Italy: Reggio Children. [http://zerosei.comune.re.it]

Gandini, L., Hill, L., Cadwell, L., and Schwall, C. (Eds) (2005): *In the Spirit of the Studio: Learning from the Atelier of Reggio Emilia.* New York: Teachers College Press.

Oken-Wright, P., and Gravett, M., (2002): Big Ideas and the Essence of Intent, in *Teaching and Learning: Collaborative Exploration of the Reggio Emilia Approach.* Fu, V., Stremmel, A., and Hill, L. (Eds). Upper Saddle River, NJ: Merrill Prentice Hall.

References

1. The 10 Best Schools in the World, and What We Can Learn from Them, *Newsweek*, December 2, 1991, pp50–59.

2. Gardner, H. (1998): Complementary Perspectives on Reggio Emilia, in *The Hundred Languages of Children: The Reggio Emilia Approach-Advanced Reflections*. Edwards, C., Gandini, L., and Forman, G. (Eds). Norwood, N.J.: Ablex, ppxvi.

3. *ibid*, pxv.

4. Gandini, L. (2004): Foundations of the Reggio Emilia Approach, in *Next Steps Toward Teaching the Reggio Way: Accepting the Challenge to Change*. Hendrick, J. (Ed). Upper Saddle River, N.J.: Pearson/Merrill Prentice Hall, 2004, p16.

5. *ibid*, p18.

6. Katz, L. (1994): Images from the World: Study Seminar on the Experience of the Municipal Infant-Toddler Centers and Preprimary Schools of Reggio Emilia, Italy, in *Reflections on the Reggio Emilia Approach*. Katz, L., and Cesarone, B. (Eds). Urbana, IL: ERIC, p12.

7. Project Zero and Reggio Children, (2001): *Making Learning Visible: Children As Individual and Group Learners*. Reggio Emilia, Italy: Reggio Children, p292.

8. Forman, G., and Fyfe, B: Negotiated Learning through Design, Documentation, and Discourse, in *Hundred Languages of Children*. Edwards, C., Gandini, L., and Forman, G. (Eds), p240.

9. Jones, E., and Nimmo, J. (1994): *Emergent Curriculum*. NAEYC.

10. For more about the investigation, see Pam Oken-Wright: Embracing Snow, in *Next Steps Toward Teaching the Reggio Way*. Hendrick, J. (Ed), pp175–96.

Chapter 11

Third Culture Kids and the PYP

Steven Carber

International school students often keep their paper citizenship but lose their cultural one. They may be good global citizens, but they don't really know what it means to be a citizen of their own country. Their internationally mobile experiences create a 'Third Culture'. This third culture involves several facets that need to be understood, addressed and supported by PYP practitioners. This chapter identifies the key elements of internationally-mobile students in international schools, and then discusses how we can support them in practice. It is hoped that many future graduate students and educators will put the ideas herein to the test of behavioral scientific methods and action research, to help establish a larger literature base about what really works in schools when it comes to helping Third Culture Kids thrive and feel as comfortable as possible.

First, a few comments about terms are important. Some readers may have wondered about the term 'Third Culture Kids' (TCKs), coined several decades ago by Useem and Downie.[1] The word 'kid' may appear a bit colloquial, and may conjure up related terms that are perhaps a bit derogatory, such as 'military brats'. This chapter does, however, use the term TCK, recognizing the important contributions that Useem made to the topic and the fact that this has become an important keyword for online searches.

Occasionally, this chapter also substitutes the pleasant phrase 'internationally mobile students', a term which may have been coined by Gerner et al[2] or one of their predecessors. Internationally mobile students and TCKs are understood here as those who live abroad for a period of time with their parents or with a single parent or guardian. Their cultural identity is then neither fully that of their home country, nor of their parent(s), nor of the host country, but it is rather a blend of many influences.

Some aspects of this discussion also apply to adult teachers who teach in several countries. We might hereby coin a new term, 'Third Culture Teachers' (TCTs), if someone has not done so already. To cite just one example of the parallels that exist between TCTs and TCKs, teachers who have taught abroad sometimes report great adjustment challenges when trying to return, and adapt, to teaching in their home country's national education system.

A significant number of readers of this book may in fact be teachers in national public school systems, in which some campuses have adopted the PYP. For them, we should affirm the thought that they probably teach some students with 'TCK' traits too. For example, in a certain internationally-themed public school in the United States, one would find half or more of the students to have parents of two different birth-nationalities. A key question in such settings is how to achieve, in a non-contrived manner, a truly international milieu despite the tendency of pop culture to make things feel monocultural.

The context of the international school and its students

International schools enrol students of numerous nationalities, many of whom may have made several transitions, as well as many host nation students who may also be faced with transitions throughout their lives. In a school it is easy enough to list nationalities, and even to benefit from the breadth of experience they bring, without being fully aware of the full impact of moves on students' emotions and their sense of identity. International schools can be melting pots in which cultures blend smoothly, or sometimes a mixed salad in which their cultures remain distinct. Some schools might be a bit of both.

In any case, teachers should consider some of the characteristics of internationally mobile students in their classrooms. First, to reiterate the above, these students have a new international 'third' culture. They are part of an international milieu that draws elements from many cultures, and that also incorporates a 'culture of transitions' – the experiences that they all share as friends move in and out of their schools.

Furthermore, these students, within their diversity, may still share many traits in common. Literature has pointed out that they may have more in common with one another, regardless of nationality, than with non-TCKs from their own country. They can feel more comfortable with other TCKs who share their international experience.[3] Although international school students assimilate influences from each culture into their life experience, their sense of identification and comfort can be strongest with other children that have similarly attended international schools in several countries.

Because these students have this new culture, they are less 'American', 'Scottish', 'Japanese', whatever, than their peers back home. When they go back to Canada or Thailand they feel less Canadian or Thai, but are also much more aware of issues of culture and nationality than some of their non-travelling counterparts.

According to Kidd and Lankenau, TCKs returning to their homeland may not feel as if they completely fit in there.[4] They might have missed learning customs of their home country and may feel most comfortable in their uniquely-created third culture. Kidd and Lankenau elaborate on the notion of feeling oneself to be marginalized between cultures, related to Schaetti's description of feeling 'at home nowhere' with a sense of 'falling off the edge of the cultural mainstream'.[5]

What, then, is K-6 culture?

In light of all of the discussion of 'culture' herein, we should consider: what is culture for a primary school-aged child? Just as educators try to create text-rich environments in the lower grades, we should create a culture-rich environment throughout the school – another reason that consideration of the above question is important. We might for a moment step back from the rich notion of culture that we get from French and Bell's popular iceberg model.[6] The food they eat, the music they know, children's literature and fairy tales that they like – all of these may be elements of culture for a fourth-grader. Culture for elementary school children may also involve participating in regional practices, such as British students going to bonfires on Bonfire Night, or Chinese students sharing Spring Festival with their extended family.

In considering *what culture is* for elementary students, we note that the diverse children in international schools haven't all watched the same TV programs (although as I write this they probably know *High School Musical* by heart!). This reminds us of Bourdieu and Passeron's notion of *Cultural Capital*, that collected cultural knowledge that tends to lend influence and status in the world.[7]

We collect it over a lifetime, and it flows in part from where we happen to have lived. I can engage in a chat about Davos or Raclette only because I happened to have lived in Switzerland; otherwise I would be silent and on the margins of such a conversation. Among friends this may not be a big deal, but among professional adults it could be important when trying to seal a business transaction over dinner. For children, cultural capital may pertain to things like making friends easily.

Relatedly, international school students haven't all played the same sports, children's activities, or music. For example, in our international schools we might encounter an American who doesn't know about baseball. With a bit of thought we can pick out baseball-like cultural benchmarks from our own culture, but it may be very difficult to understand these cultural benchmarks for all of our students. For example, having unfortunately never lived in Korea, I know little about Korean culture, so I find it difficult to prepare my Korean students for assimilating when they return home.

Positive aspects of TCKs

The intent of this chapter is to help the unfamiliar reader better understand the TCK population, and the discussion may as well serve to re-orientate the familiar reader. We review the positives first as a reminder that most TCKs tend to do well eventually, and that they have many advantages in becoming 'global citizens'. International exposure at an early age appears to have an enduring impact that shapes both children and adults. Most of them are positive, and many encourage traits of the IB learner profile.

Several studies suggest that TCKs acquire many positive traits. Iwama found TCKs to have more self-confidence and flexible thinking than their non-TCK counterparts.[8] Internationally mobile students are also said to develop sophisticated observation skills, respect diversity, and exemplify multicultural education paradigms due to their heightened pluralistic world-view.[9] According to Gillies[10] and Gerner *et al*,[11] international school students tend to grow up bilingual or multilingual, thereby granting them an exceptional openness to foreign languages and cultures.

Furthermore, international school students may be of great interest to the future global political and economic climate, as they have 'greater interest in maintaining geographically mobile lives and orientation to international careers'.[12] Living internationally can lead to difficulties but it can also create greater mental health as youngsters learn that they can cope.[13]

TCK's development of pluralist world-views and respect for diversity fosters the open-minded qualities of the international citizen reflected in the IB learner profile that is highly important for the complexities of today's geo-political world.

Negative aspects of the TCK experience

The above qualities do not develop without potential challenges: Werkman, Farley, Butler, and Quayhagen suggest that 'geographical change has been shown to be related to increased incidence rates of a variety of psychiatric disorders in adults, including alcoholism and family disorganization'.[14] Öry, Simons, Verhulst, Leenders, and Wolters also linked international moves, especially returns to the homeland, to depression among some internationally mobile children.[15]

Additionally, Haour-Knipe reminded readers that international moves may exacerbate adolescent identity crisis and rebellion against parents.[16] Öry *et al* note that research has documented culture shock in adults, and limited literature also notes the possibility of acculturative stress in children.[17] Haour-Knipe illuminates challenges for migrating youngsters when she writes, 'Acculturating to the beliefs, values, and basic way of life of the host culture usually means abandoning old ways, a process often accompanied by unease, a sense of guilt, and some sense of loss of identity'.[18]

Internationally-mobile students may experience acculturative stress, articulated by Sandhu and Asrabadi as a combination of homesickness, fear, and communication challenges.[19] Furthermore, relocation contributes potentially to homesickness and to the 'interruption of routines and habits together with a likely change in perceived role and sense of self'.[20]

What do we do to help?

As noted in the chapter introduction, this may be the most important section of our discussion – the action component! The dialogue that emerges around this set of ideas constitutes something for schools and families to actually *do*. But the 'action plan' is not entirely clear or finalized. Among the important tasks that remain for the current and future generations of PYP practitioners is appropriately putting these and other approaches to the tests of behavioral science/educational research/action research to see if the following three categories of action really *help* students:

1. *Help students settle and with their transition into the school.*

Adults encountering TCKs can assist their transitions by creating environments within peer groups where they can share their concerns with others and realize that what they are experiencing is normal. As Kidd and Lankenau note: 'Strive to help the students feel a part of the class and school. Implement strategies such as the buddy/mentor system and cooperative learning activities to give newcomers opportunities to interact with other students. Encourage them to become involved in school activities.'[21]

Upon new students' arrival, educators and students should talk things through. When children enter their environment, we should facilitate adjustment by discussing feelings and reactions with family members and with other people who have been through a similar transition. Schools should train school counseling staff in the methods endorsed by the currently limited body of research literature on effective interventions for TCK discomfort.

2. Establish a culture-rich environment.

International school teachers do, and should, strive to create a comfortable environment. Small details like carpeted reading corners with diverse literature, bean bags and living room-like lamps make a classroom more inviting to newcomers.

PYP teachers can also leverage inquiry-based instruction to honor the backgrounds of individual students: when students are asked to identify questions of genuine interest to them (which may lead to 'student question projects'), encourage questions related to the children's nationalities, backgrounds, and home cultures.

Teachers can open up cultural issues explicitly – use metacognition to help students develop their identities. As Kidd and Lankenau suggest: 'Foster students' multicultural identities. As the multicultural dimensions of classrooms and schools are explored and celebrated, raise awareness of the diversity that TCKs bring to schools.'[22] Finally, work on decision-making skills. In-class opportunities to reinforce good decision-making skills are helpful to those making cultural transitions.

The following are anecdotes collected from international schools that hint at the type of culture-rich classroom activities that might be viewed as 'on the right track', followed by a comment on why we would want to do things like these:

A new student from Sicily had a parent who was a well-renowned chef and baker. The parent came into the class for several sessions and taught all the students how to make bread dough and bake bread in a Sicilian style. This was in conjunction with a unit about how people grow and get their food to survive. (We might do this sort of thing with intent to foster understanding and appreciation of home cultures.)

A school on the US West Coast enrolled several students with Chinese heritage. During a unit on Chinese culture, a 13-year-old published author from a nearby town was invited to visit the school with her mother to present to the class about her book entitled *Kids like me in China*.[23] The author was an inspirational hit with the children, and she signed copies of the book for all. (We might do this sort of thing with intent to prompt reflection about how we are similar and different to those we left behind in our previous homes.)

During one school's Schoolwide Enrichment Model clusters,[24] course offerings during the school day included Taiko drumming, French language, and anthropology, to name a few. (We might do this sort of thing with an intent to provide a rich variety of cultural experiences that honor and augment the diversity within our TCK populations.)

A teacher in one PYP school held weekly creative drama sessions in which students acted out scenes around the theme of adapting to procedures and customs of the host country. These ranged from things like buying a train ticket through a thick glass window, entering a 'closed circle' of potential friends on the playground, and checking out at the grocery store. Attention was given to being non-offensive and non-generalizing, while still attending to the potential humor in these situations when in a new country. (We might do this sort of thing with intent to lessen culture shock and acculturative stress.)

PYP teachers around the world can surely add many more rich items to a list such as the one above.

3. Help students' transition out of the school/return home.

Returning home can be challenging for TCKs, as individuals begin to feel the cultural gap between themselves and people from the home country. As McNichol stated about one such international journeyer: '[ask him] ...about the political situation in Eastern Africa and the 23-year-old computer instructor has no trouble ... but turn to more mundane topics – an old *M*A*S*H* episode, say, or the ruckus over New versus Classic Coke and [this American] draws a blank.'[25] These are slightly dated examples, but PYP teachers could cite various similar cultural and political phenomena for current generations and countries.

They may also note that in the era of Facebook and YouTube it is easier to check up on pop culture phenomena. (Not to suggest that over-identification with any region's pop culture is necessarily desirable or helpful, but maybe a crash course in this sort of thing for each new country in the student's experience could aid in feeling more comfortable there.)

The following are some suggestions for schools in regard to supporting students' moves home: First, 'provide support for academic transitions. TCKs may need additional support in academic areas that may differ in other countries or schools'.[26] This could be especially urgent for students who move from, say, a PYP environment to a 'drill and practice' type setting or a new language environment. Parents can take a lead role here, perhaps by obtaining examples of workbooks from the new country, and of course by selecting the best possible school with, as close as possible, a similar philosophy.

Second, discuss students' expectations for returning home. Manage reverse culture shock in children by discussing it and preparing them for it. Thirdly, if feasible, and if students seem comfortable with it, pair a soon-departing student with a newly-arrived student from the same country. This could be as simple as holding a one-time 'lunch bunch' in which 'What's currently popular in...' and related topics are discussed with adult guidance. Finally, with parent permission and supervision, keep students connected with previous peer groups using web-based tools such as Facebook, Skype, and email.

A transdisciplinary curriculum

When students are studying a PYP transdisciplinary theme such as 'where we are in place and time', this should connect with their own third culture location and time. Every year PYP students should understand better 'where they are'. For a TCK, this may mean looking at how their third culture relates to other aspects of the world they are studying. They need to make connections between their third culture and what they study. This includes developing a strong understanding of their home culture, their host culture, and that of their peers.

That is among the reasons why we generally don't do a unit purely on 'Ancient Egypt' but instead look at how ancient civilizations help us understand who we are and where we came from. The student from Ethiopia might report on the anthropological importance of the Coptic language in conjunction with the Rosetta Stone, while the student from France may want to know why a giant obelisk ended up in Paris. In encouraging these kinds of student inquiries, though, teachers should be aware that students might not have much direct experience and knowledge of their home country. They may only have visited it on vacation. Teachers may have to be 'inquirers' and find out about the culture of their students themselves so that they can incorporate it properly into their classrooms.

Beyond the transdisciplinary themes, the key concepts of change, connection, perspective, responsibility and reflection seem to be words that genuinely apply to the international sojourner's life. These are concepts worth talking about frequently with students. Surely the reader could elaborate on personal change based on time in other countries. Connection in this context could relate to how the TCK remains connected in some ways to mom's culture, dad's culture, and the host country culture.

Perspectives change as we compare traditions and practices in new countries of residence to how things were done in our previous home. Responsibility may relate to respecting and caring for the host country and friends' cultural perspectives; children generally become increasingly responsible TCKs as they spend more time in the global environment. Finally, reflection and metacognition may help sort through emotions connected to phenomena like culture shock and missing friends.

PYP educators may be able to deliberately leverage the 'lines of inquiry' and 'teacher questions/provocations' elements of the planner to tap below the protective layer that often hides students' rich international experiences. For example, even though we learn in PYP training that central ideas and maybe even guiding questions should not be too case-specific, they can invite case-specific individual inquiries from any student's background: what do people do when they don't have enough water resources to meet demand? The student from California could report on canal diversion projects for Los Angeles, while the Cypriot student could report on desalination facilities near Larnaca.

Both students can meaningfully connect with their place(s) of origin, however unfamiliar to them. Meanwhile, students from water-rich countries also learn from other perspectives. The above inquiries are offered as slightly simplified examples; ultimately we should consider what is relevant to a ten-year-old; the frame of reference should include students' backgrounds.

The 'what resources need to be gathered' phase of planning could also be put to work to address the pluralistic worldviews, backgrounds, and cultural identifications of TCKs. When one searches children's books on the most popular online booksellers, with a little bit of investigation one can find related books from countries other than the US, Canada, and the UK (and let's face it, a disproportionate number of our resources are sometimes ordered from these places). If we go to the same company's German subsidiary, (the web address ends in .de) and enter 'Wasser', we see many water resource books in German.

Furthermore, in the PYP planner resources section we might also list people, so it would be a good time to invite in the mom from Bolivia who once worked at a Bolivian water reclamation plant. Interestingly, the above discussion about how to honor the diversity of TCKs in our classroom is beginning to relate to another hot question in our field right now: what exactly *is* an international education? See the above, and please invent and share more ideas along these lines!

Finally, of course, the PYP invites attention to the IB learner profile. The PYP intends that students become inquirers, knowledgeable, thinkers, communicators, principled, open-minded, caring, risk-takers, balanced, and reflective. These terms may at first glance seem to have little to do specifically with internationalism or third culture kids, but the IB suggests that they characterize the types of internationally-minded students that are to be nurtured in IB schools, and that might be called *internationalists*.[27]

In schools with large TCK populations, some of these traits can sometimes flow quite naturally within the school milieu, whereas in some public national-system PYP schools there may or may not be as much inherent diversity (in some cases, there may be more). As an open-ended question for the reader, in what ways does the TCK experience relate to the above components of the PYP learner profile? And in what ways can nurturing and practicing these habits of being actually help achieve greater comfort within the TCK's experience?

These may be great questions to guide someone's MEd program papers. It seems a bit much to explain each of the profile items one by one in light of the international sojourner's experience, but let us take a couple of examples: we become better *communicators* when we move to different countries, because we have to learn the nuances and, hopefully, the languages of that place. We increase our ability to be *reflective* because we now think more about how things are done differently here and there and what the advantages are of each approach. Of course we also *take risks* upon moving to a new place, but we usually come out all the better for it.

Conclusion

TCKs have a distinct culture. They can be very successful, and may reflect many positive values that articulate with the IB learner profile. There are some difficulties that might be alleviated through ideas like some of those above.

However, in order to best care for internationally-mobile students, educators, schools, and universities with an interest in international education need to expand the research base into the TCK phenomenon. For the moment we might need to rely on suppositions about what might help, but various interventions should, in the coming years, be investigated with solid research designs that will give PYP teachers increased confidence when choosing various approaches. This author and others may be willing to discuss ideas for such studies with graduate students considering topics for their theses.

Above all, international schools should support families and students. A close family unit makes a big difference – possibly an internationally mobile student's only stability. The students that these families enroll bring a wide variety of perspectives, experience and cultural richness to a school and they are the reason that we do what we do. The good news here, and a fitting ending point, is that the PYP is already perhaps the best framework in the world for supporting the TCK's development, and with a bit of thoughtful leveraging of the elements of the programme, PYP teachers can help internationally mobile students to thrive.

References

1. Useem, R., and Downie, R.D. (1976): Third-culture kids, in *Today's Education*, 65(3), pp103-105.

2. Gerner, M., Perry, F., Moselle, M.A., and Archibold, M. (1992): Characteristics of internationally mobile adolescents, in *Journal of School Psychology*, 30(2), pp197-214.

3. Storti, C. (1997): *The Art of coming home*. Boston: Intercultural Press.

4. Kidd, J.K., and Lankenau, L.L. (n.d.): Third culture kids: Returning to their passport country, retrieved December 15, 2008, from: www.state.gov/m/dghr/flo/c22473.htm

5. Schaetti, B., as cited in Kidd, J.K., and Lankenau, L.L. (n.d.): Third culture kids: Returning to their passport country, retrieved December 15, 2008 from: www.state.gov/m/dghr/flo/c22473.htm

6. French, W.L., and Bell, C.H. (1978): *Organization development*. New Jersey: Prentice Hall.

7. Bourdieu, P., and Passeron, J.C. (1990): *Reproduction in Education, Society and Culture*. Thousand Oaks: Sage.

8. Iwama, H.F. (1990): *Factors influencing transculturation of Japanese overseas teenagers*. Unpublished Doctor of Philosophy Dissertation, Graduate School, College of Education, Pennsylvania State University, USA.

9. Useem, R., and Downie, R.D. (1976): Third-culture kids, in *Today's Education*, 65(3), pp103-105.

10. Gillies, W.D. (1998): Children on the move: Third culture kids, in *Childhood Education*, 75(1), pp36-38.

11. Gerner, M., Perry, F., Moselle, M.A., and Archibold, M. (1992): Characteristics of Internationally Mobile adolescents, in *Journal of School Psychology*, 30(2), pp197-214.

12. Werkman, S.L., as cited in Gerner, M., and Perry, F. (2000): Gender differences in cultural acceptance and career orientation among internationally mobile and non-internationally mobile adolescents, in *School Psychology Review*, 29(2), p267.

13. Gerner, M., and Perry, F. (2000): Gender differences in cultural acceptance and career orientation among internationally mobile and non-internationally mobile adolescents, in *School Psychology Review*, 29(2), pp267-83.

14. Werkman, S.L., Farley, G.K., Butler, C., and Quayhagen, M. (1981): The psychological effects of moving and living overseas, in *Journal of the American Academy of Child Psychiatry*, 20(3), p646.

15. Öry, F.G., Simons, M., Verhulst, F.C., Leenders, F.H., and Wolters, W.G. (1991): Children who cross cultures, in *Social Science Medicine*, 32(1), pp29-34.

16. Haour-Knipe, M. (1989): International employment and children: Geographical mobility and mental health among children of professionals, in *Social Science Medicine*, 28(3), pp197-205.

17. Oberg, K. (1960): Cultural shock: Adjustment to new cultural environments, in *Practical Anthropology*, 7, pp177-182; and Haour-Knipe, M. (1989): International employment and children: Geographical mobility and mental health among children of professionals, in *Social Science Medicine*, 28(3), pp197-205.

18. Haour-Knipe, M. (1989): p.203.

19. Sandhu, D.S., and Asrabadi, B.R. (1994): Development of an acculturative stress scale for international students. Preliminary findings, in *Psychological Reports*, 75(2), pp435-448.

20. Bell, J., and Bromnick, R. (1998): Young people in transition: The relationship between homesickness and self disclosure, in *Journal of Adolescence*, 21(6), p745.

21. Kidd, J.K., and Lankenau, L.L. (n.d.): Third culture kids: Returning to their passport country, retrieved December 15, 2008 from: www.state.gov/m/dghr/flo/c22473.htm

22. *ibid.*

23. Fry, Y.Y. (2001): *Kids like me in China*. St. Paul, MN: Yeong & Yeong Book Company.

24. Renzulli, J.S., and Reis, S. M. (2002): What is schoolwide enrichment? How gifted programs relate to total school improvement, in *Gifted Child Today*, 25(4), pp18-25, 64.

25. McNichol, T. (1991): The wanderers, in *In Health*, 34(4), p34.

26. Kidd, J.K., and Lankenau, L.L. (n.d.): Third culture kids: Returning to their passport country, retrieved December 15, 2008 from: www.state.gov/m/dghr/flo/c22473.htm

27. International Baccalaureate Organization (2000): *Making the PYP happen*. Cardiff: IBO, p3.

Chapter 12

What will characterize international education in public schools?

Steven Carber

This chapter is based on a reprint of an article from the April 2009 issue of the *Journal of Research in International Education*: Carber, S. (2009): 'What will characterize international education in US public schools?' *Journal of Research in International Education*, 8(1), 100-110.

The author thanks Sage publications and the *JRIE* for their reprint permission. The text has been slightly modified from its original format, with permission, in order to match a book format versus a journal format. Although the discussion centers on public schools in the USA (where the PYP has seen rapid growth), PYP practitioners may find some of the ideas applicable to schools in other settings. The original article was completed in 2006, so some citations may reference documents that have since been released in newer editions.

Introduction

The present discussion proposes strategies for offering an international education in US public schools, drawing on the milieus, curricula and accreditation standards established by the broad family of overseas schools known as 'international schools'. Such considerations are timely in the current era of globalization and in light of the ongoing need to nurture an internationally-minded leadership base for the future. This discussion includes a call for interested educators to further discuss and refine models of international public schooling. While this text is focused on US public school settings, the broader readership of this chapter may contribute to the ongoing dialogue about this topic, and may appropriately adapt emerging models to other national settings.

Whatever the answer to the guiding question for this chapter, it is reasonable to suggest that an informed internationally-oriented program should be envisioned for *all* public school students in the global era, in keeping with Suarez-Orozco's[1] reminders of a world of increasing international complexity, and with Stewart and Kagan's[2] call to develop public international education models to counter the 'time warp' from which US education standards and issues often flow.

Many US schools are taking an interest in fostering an international identity, as illustrated by the list in Figure 1, which was compiled from a simple web search of US public schools with the word 'international' or 'global' within their names. This author does not claim to know a great deal about each of the schools located

Figure 1 – *United States Public and Public Charter Schools with 'International' or Related Terms in Their Names*

Park International Magnet School (Arkansas)
International School of Monterey (California)
Bloomfield School of Global Studies (California)
Academy International Elementary School (Colorado)
Midland International Elementary School (Colorado)
Sabin International School (Colorado)
International School at Rogers Magnet (Connecticut)
International School at Dundee (Connecticut)
Carlos Rosario International School (District of Columbia)
Freedom 7 Elementary School of International Studies (Florida)
Williams Middle Magnet School for International Affairs (Florida)
International Community School (Georgia)
Snowden International School (Massachusetts)
International Academy (Michigan)
Harbor City International School (Minnesota)
Rosa International Middle School (New Jersey)
Baccalaureate School for Global Education (New York)
Winthrow International High School (Ohio)
Tri County International Academy (Ohio)
Eisenhower International School (Oklahoma)
Eugene International High School (Oregon)
John Stanford International School (Oregon)
Upper St Clair International School (Pennsylvania)
Zundy Junior High International Academy (Texas)
Westchester Academy for International Studies (Texas)
John Stanford International School (Washington)

through this general web search, but the number of public schools now giving a nod to internationalism may hint at the importance of this text.

In many independent international schools abroad, 'internationalism' is simply part of the milieu, as diverse clusters of bilingual or multilingual students from many different countries 'hang out' together on the playground and discuss topics like living abroad during parents' diplomatic assignments, or how the sun never sets in June in their Finnish friend's home region, or any number of other interesting topics.

But what if most of a school's students are from the local neighborhood, generally watching the same local television broadcasts and shopping at the same megamarkets, even during summer vacation? What if economic restraints or routine prevent many of their families or school classes from traveling very far beyond their own state or town? Can educators in such settings genuinely create playground or classroom milieus that approximate those found at overseas private international schools? Questions abound.

It is the intent of this chapter, again, to open a dialogue about international school identity questions in a decade in which public schools in many states and countries are taking a keen interest in nurturing globally-minded students. The following discussion addresses the notion of an international student profile, followed by a lengthier discussion of relevant accreditation standards and what aspiring international schools might *do* to address these standards.

An international student profile

A key to any school's identity is the question 'what kind of student do we wish to graduate?' The IB learner profile purports to characterize the international student. At first glance, the terms caring, communicator, inquirer, knowledgeable, open-minded, principled, reflective, risk-taker, thinker, and balanced may not seem to have much to do specifically with internationalism, but the IB suggests that these terms characterize the types of students that are nurtured in IB schools.

Says the IB: 'The attempt to define the ideal of internationalism in ever clearer terms and the struggle to move closer to that ideal are central to the mission of their internationally oriented schools. Furthermore, the learner profile, which can be regarded as a set of dispositions evidenced by external behaviour, articulates 'the kind of student who we hope to graduate… the kind of person we would proudly call an internationalist'.[3]

Not all international schools offer one or more of the three IB programmes (PYP, Middle Years Programme [MYP] and Diploma Programme [DP]), but the IB learner profile may be an important preliminary consideration for any school aspiring to an international identity.[4] Non-IB international schools may choose to create their own original set of student descriptors.

International accreditation

In 2003, the Council of International Schools (CIS) and the New England Association for Schools and Colleges (NEASC) released the seventh edition of their, *Guide to School Evaluation and Accreditation*,[5] which has been used in US public school joint-accreditation self-study and team visitation processes. CIS is headquartered in the UK, with accreditation offices in Spain. This organization offers a variety of services to international schools, their faculty members, and their students. CIS conducts joint accreditation visits with US regional accreditation agencies such as the New England Association of Schools and Colleges (NEASC), the Southern Association of Colleges and Schools (SACS), and the Western Association of School and Colleges (WASC).

These regional accreditation agencies are among six such regional agencies in the USA. The seventh edition accreditation document provides helpful guidance for schools aspiring to be internationally minded. One of the guiding principles of the seventh edition is that a school's philosophy should be oriented to the United Nations Universal Declaration of Human Rights (UNDHR). In comparison to some independent schools with admissions screening, public international schools will be, whether they articulate it or not, uniquely dedicated to the UNDHR's call for equitable education for *all* children, whether wealthy or economically disadvantaged.

CIS accreditation through joint visits with regional associations could assist US public schools in solidifying their international school identity, in addition to the usual self-improvement benefits of the accreditation process. Accredited CIS schools can take advantage of other CIS initiatives, like the International Student Award[6] which could further help schools establish a clearer international school orientation.

Perhaps CIS scholarships can someday be established to allow some deserving public school students to travel abroad for the many CIS, or other international school sporting events, or other competitions. Teachers from one international public charter school in California were among the first US public school faculty members to be flown to the European Council of International Schools' (ECIS) November educators' conferences in Europe, which helped connect that school to a broader international community.

CIS accreditation standard A5 states that 'the school's Philosophy and Objectives shall commit the school to promoting international and inter-cultural experiences for students'.[7] So, any aspiring public international school will want to make its international emphasis explicit in its philosophy and objectives statement. The following excerpt is an example of how this has been done in one setting:

> The school expands educational opportunities for children in the country by bringing world-class international education – typical of exemplary overseas independent schools – to a public school setting. The school mission statement's emphasis on 'caring, conscientious, and compassionate' global citizens is consistent with the United Nations Declaration of Human Rights and its 'promotion of universal respect' and 'development of friendly relations' between all people. Beyond instilling international mindedness in its own students, the school works to inspire all children and the broader community by promoting awareness of other countries, languages, and cultures in highly active and visible ways.[8]

A school's identity and purpose flows from its philosophy and objectives statement, and indeed, regional and international accreditation cannot easily proceed without having one in place. A school's identity starts here.

Another relevant CIS standard for accreditation comes from section G5: 'The school shall actively promote intercultural and international awareness.'[9] What practices, emphases and programs might a school have in place to do this? The following seven sections of this text, with headings created by the author, summarize some possibilities in this regard.

Foreign language instruction

Foreign language instruction for all grade levels should *not* be, as some prospective families might assume, the key identifier of an international school – rather, it is simply one of several. However, the importance of K-12 second language instruction in North America, especially in the USA, should not be underestimated. During the author's overseas teaching experiences, it was common to find elementary school students who were multilingual, often in their mothers' first language, their fathers' different first language, the language of their non-English speaking host country, and English or another international school language of instruction.

Indeed, several of the author's expatriate friends enrolled their preschool children in host country public schools simply to allow them to absorb the local language. The author taught for several years in US public schools, and noted in such settings the relative absence of multilingual students, with occasional exceptions.

In light of the relative lack of foreign-language training in the USA, innovative US public international schools should establish a precedent for K-12 foreign-language instruction, especially in widely spoken languages such as Mandarin. Boufis[10] cites five schools that claim great benefits after initiating Mandarin instruction. Chmelynski[11] mentions model Mandarin programs in Chicago and federal Mandarin support such as a grant to the Portland Public Schools from the US Defense Department. Schools seeking guidance for how to implement a new Mandarin program may find guidance from Huang[12] who explains a content based approach used in Canada.

Genuine student interactions with varied cultures/nations

Student interactions with other cultures or nations should be genuine, frequent and should not be oriented too much towards Begler's 'five Fs' – food, festivals, fashion, famous people and folklore.[13] There is nothing wrong with International Food Day, but taking a class on a field trip to a Chinese school in San Francisco's Chinatown, 'pen-paling' with a school in Miami's Little Havana, or going on a campout and hike in the Navajo Nation may be more representative of the type of international activities that will address standard G5 in an international public school setting.

Some other relevant activities that the author has witnessed in public school settings include making 1000 paper cranes for the Hiroshima Peace Park; selling hot chocolate to benefit the Heifer Project relief organization; collecting hygiene products to be delivered to Iraqi civilians; writing to pen pals at an international school in Italy; visiting a Taoist shrine; inviting a 13-year-old Chinese-American published author to visit the school; and participating in a local university's filming of a classroom segment for a documentary on immigration.

An internationally-recognized curriculum

Schools seeking an internationally oriented curriculum might consider the IB PYP, MYP or DP. Inevitably, most public international schools will struggle with articulating their curricular choice with local state standards, which could be viewed as a creative tension rather than as a problem. These schools may want to consider adopting an international *framework* such as the PYP rather than an international *curriculum*; they may want to focus more on the *how* of teaching if they do not have as much control of the *what*.

Creating an internationally oriented school in a state standards environment certainly seems better tried than not, despite the possible friction with provincial or national assumptions and curricula. To cite a brief example of how to address these challenges, if standards mandate the teaching of the American Revolution, schools can teach this as a single case study of the wider theme of *revolutions*, which may have a universally relevant central idea like 'People are sometimes willing to fight or die to change political systems'. Other countries' revolutions can be studied within that unit too.

Whatever internationally recognized curricula schools adopt, these will ideally be infused with the notions of inquiry-based instruction and Teaching for Understanding, both of which are now common (and interrelated) models in many excellent overseas international schools and in recognized international curricula. Short[14] offers excellent overviews of inquiry for the aspiring international school, and Harvard's annual Project Zero summer institutes offer training in Teaching for Understanding.[15]

Overseas experienced teachers

Schools of excellence should seek out overseas experienced teachers. These teachers' range of perspectives and international anecdotes broaden students' classroom experiences. Teachers from overseas international schools who return to their English-speaking homelands may be a targeted group of candidates within internationally oriented US public school settings. A few US public schools, or public school recruiting organizations, have begun to attend international school job fairs like those run by CIS, International Schools Services and Search Associates. The public international school will face the challenge of offering attractive packages to these teachers who may have received subsidized housing or tax-free income situations abroad.

Commitment to UNDHR and visible respect for diversity

Visible respect for diversity goes hand-in-hand with a commitment to the UNDHR. The IB PYP has used a teacher reflection survey in some of its training sessions entitled 'How International is my School?' and it includes several items that point to this respect for diversity. These include:

1. the school's culture accommodates, reflects and takes positive advantage of the cultures represented in the school;

2. the school takes positive advantage of the diversity within the student body to enrich the learning and lives of the whole school community; and

3. the adults in the school community actively model intercultural understanding.

Descriptors such as these are rated on a 1-4 scale. Most importantly, beyond a school scoring high on such a survey, the school's students should be seen treating each other with respect on the playground and throughout the school, as would be expected in any school of excellence.

International exchange programs

A limited amount of literature supports the benefits of student exchange programs between US public schools and public schools in other countries. Zsiray *et al*[16] describe a successful ongoing exchange program between a public high school in Utah, USA, and a state high school in Moscow, Russia. Freberg[17] reminds readers that hosting international students is a meaningful experience for students and families who may not have enough money to study abroad themselves. Mathiesen and Lager[18] present a model for international student exchanges with an emphasis on long-term friendships and tolerance.

While students at private international schools may think nothing about jumping on a train for a weekend family trip to a neighboring country, many US public school students lack similar opportunities. International exchange programs might alleviate US students' lack of experiences abroad, and websites such as Studyabroad.com[19] can assist in the location of suitable programs.

Bringing an appendix forward

The CIS Seventh Edition guide provides an excellent list of mechanisms for addressing standard G5, and this list should not be overlooked despite its placement as an appendix at the very end of the accreditation self-study document. The following list includes some excerpts from the 18-point list:

- Deliver the teaching/learning programme through more than one language.
- Introduce international/intercultural aspects into curricular and co-curricular programmes in as many areas as possible (especially social sciences, language and culture, arts and music courses).
- Use recruitment policies aimed at creating national, linguistic and cultural diversity within the staff.
- Encourage foreign students to join the school, either on a medium term basis or on short visits.
- Encourage students to travel abroad on educational trips and/or exchanges.
- Invite speakers and performers from abroad and from other cultural groups.
- Encourage students and teachers to establish joint projects (online and other) with schools abroad.

- Encourage teachers to pursue visits, exchanges and professional development activities abroad.

- Involve students in community service abroad through fundraising and/or practical tasks.

- Ensure the school library/media center provides students with access to information and leisure sources from more than one culture and in more than one language.[20]

Summary

It is the hope of the author that this article stimulates further discussion on the questions and themes raised herein. Additional ideas and questions already come to mind – what if, for example, public funds do not easily allow the public international school to build the excellent school library noted in the last bullet point above?

Can public international schools in certain areas, in the light of limited per capita state education expenditures and the commendable mandate to educate all students, ever look and feel like prominent independent schools such as those accredited abroad by CIS? Do readers have additional ideas to offer to this discussion?

In a recent compelling article, Bartlett and Tangye[21] proposed a new set of standards by which to evaluate internationalism, and called for a genuine debate on the meaning of internationalism in education. Readers might furthermore consider the possibility of a new regional association or affiliation of public international schools. The true conclusion to this article may well lie in the debate that emerges from such interaction, which can only be helpful in promoting internationalism within the US public school context.

References

1. Suarez-Orozco, M.M. (2005): Rethinking education in the global era, in *Phi Delta Kappan*, 87(3), pp209–212.

2. Stewart, V., and Kagan, S.L. (2005): Conclusion: new world view: education in a global era, in *Phi Delta Kappan*, 87(3), pp241–5.

3. International Baccalaureate Organization, (2000): *Making the PYP Happen*. Cardiff: IBO, p3. (Author's note: The quote is from the 2000 edition, but teachers should now be using the 2007 version.)

4. International Baccalaureate Organization, (2008): www.ibo.org (as retrieved on 25 February 2008).

5. Percy, G., Styan, D., Galo, D., O'Donnell, R., and Woodward, P. (2003): *Guide to School Evaluation and Accreditation*, 7th edition. Hampshire: Council of International Schools.

6. Council of International Schools (2008): The international student award. Available at: www.cois.org/page.cfm?p=53 (as retrieved on 25 February 2008).

7. Percy, G., Styan, D., Galo, D., O'Donnell, R., and Woodward, P. (2003): *Guide to School Evaluation and Accreditation*, 7th edition. Hampshire: Council of International Schools, p29.

8. International School of Monterey, (2005): *Philosophy and Objectives of the International School of Monterey*. Monterey: International School of Monterey.

9. Percy, G., Styan, D., Galo, D., O'Donnell, R., and Woodward, P. (2003): *Guide to School Evaluation and Accreditation*, 7th edition. Hampshire: Council of International Schools, p91.

10. Boufis, C. (2007): The year of the Chinese language, in *Scholastic Administrator*, 7(1), pp22–6.

11. Chmelynski, C. (2005): Chinese language instruction getting more popular in public schools, in *School Board News*, 8 November, pp1–4.

12. Huang, J. (2003): Chinese as a foreign language in Canada: A content-based programme for elementary school, in *Language, Culture, and Curriculum*, 16(1), pp70–89.

13. Begler, E. (1998): Global cultures: first steps in understanding, in *Social Education*, 62(5), pp272–275.

14. Short, K. (1997): Inquiring into inquiry, in *Learning*, 25(3), pp52–54.

15. Gardner, H., and Perkins, D.N. (1988): Why zero? A brief introduction to project zero, in *The Journal of Aesthetic Education*, 22, pp7–10; (and) *Project Zero* (2008), available at: www.pz.harvard.edu/index.cfm (as retrieved on 25 February 2008).

16. Zsiray, S.W., Parse ova, M., and Eltseva, G. (2002): Lyceum 1511 and mountain crest high school, in *The Social Studies*, 93(3), pp134–7.

17. Freberg, M. (1993): Exchange programs bring the international home, in *Childhood Education*, 70(2), p96.

18. Mathiesen, S.G., and Lager, P. (2007): A model for developing international student exchanges, in *Social Work Education*, 26(3), pp280–291.

19. Studyabroad.com (2008), available at: www.studyabroad.com/highschool/ (as retrieved on 25 February 2008).

20. Percy, G., Styan, D., Galo, D., O'Donnell, R., and Woodward, P. (2003): *Guide to School Evaluation and Accreditation*, 7th edition. Hampshire: Council of International Schools, p105.

21. Bartlett, K., and Tangye, R. (2007): Defining internationalism in education through standards available at: http://intranet1.canacad.ac.jp:3445/strategic/admin/download.html?attachid=301578 (as retrieved on 1 December 2008).

Chapter 13

Quality not bureaucracy

Simon Davidson

Education today is awash with ideas like quality and excellence, for which teachers and administrators are accountable. We often face substantial pressure to produce good quality, and to demonstrate that we have done so. Most people will agree that we want high quality, not low quality. However there can be very different understandings of what this means, and how to go about getting it. I look at two possibilities.

One important view is a bureaucratic approach that became prominent in industry during the 19th and 20th centuries. Initially it was more concerned with efficiency, but it is now extended to quality, particularly a view of acceptable performance. Such models use a top-down process to define numerical goals, and to impose processes to reach these goals. This helped develop efficient factories, but can produce difficulties with quality even in manufacturing, and may be counter-productive in schools.

A more effective approach comes from the work of W Edwards Deming. His ideas underpinned much of the progress of the Japanese car industry in recent decades, and were influential to the Toyota Way[1] that contributed to Toyota becoming arguably the world's leading car manufacturer.

His ideas are more complex than mere numerical measures and targets, reflecting better the complexity of education. They point to several important areas on which to focus, including developing profound knowledge – detailed knowledge of students and their learning; concentrating on the learning process; constant improvement; and teamwork.

They also give grounds for avoiding *waste*, such as putting precious time and energy into external 'quality' procedures that are disconnected from learning processes, and point to the dangers of top-down management. Occasionally 'squelchers' would like to concentrate on these ineffective methods.

Deming's approach extends the collegiality and reflective practice that is already part of best PYP practice, increasing true quality and improving students' learning.

A bureaucratic model of quality

During the Middle Ages, goods were produced by individual craftsmen and small producers. Quality was controlled by guilds, which maintained working practices and had a system of apprenticeship and membership to ensure that everyone in a particular trade had the necessary skills and knowledge. As the industrial revolution took hold, there was a great innovation – mass production using interchangeable parts. Individual work was no longer possible, as parts had to fit together reliably. Quality meant parts were within certain tolerances. This enabled assembly-line production, with much greater productivity per worker. When one part was faulty, it could be replaced.

Large groups of workers performed similar types of work, grouped together under the supervision of a foreman who also took on the responsibility to control the quality of the work manufactured. The foreman could report up a line of command, allowing forms of organisation to be adopted from the main large organisations of the time: the military and the church.

In the early 20th century, efficiency was the main goal, not quality. Frederick Winslow Taylor investigated how one could also design more efficient production lines by measuring output.[2] His 'scientific management' approach elevated management as a separate discipline, with practices developed using methods like time and motion studies.

This was the ultimate top-down model, in which managers gave workers detailed instruction and supervision, so that they carried out discrete tasks in prescribed ways. An 'expert' designed specific processes and set clear metrics. Technicians had the required training to carry them out. An inspection process checked that technicians did their work adequately, measuring them against pre-determined goals and system.

Bureaucracy in schools

On the surface it may appear nonsensical to apply a standardisation model to children, who are clearly not a standardised product. However there were good reasons for doing so. As education developed in the 20th century, new methods were introduced that were not universally accepted. Teachers, as individual professionals, had a large amount of autonomy and often taught in isolation. There may have been great innovation in some classrooms, but a lack of consistency led to concern about overall consistency. Standardised quantitative measurement and bureaucratic measures seemed to be the most appropriate models at the time to guarantee educational outputs reliably.

Since then, standardised approaches have been introduced in many countries, with simple metrics, often highlighted in league tables. For example, Standard Assessment Tasks (SATs) play a central role in the National Curriculum of England and Wales, and there is a substantial testing component in the American *No Child Left Behind* legislation. According to this model, overall pressure for certain scores will work its way down to individual classrooms and classroom decisions that improve these scores, which are taken as the principle indicator of success.

The bureaucratic model's reliance on measurement creates problems in education, where the outcomes are complex and long-term. Some other processes are easy to measure. A McDonald's burger is a certain size and consistency, and is cooked for a certain period of time. A widget may be a particular size, weight and strength. It is harder to measure our ultimate goals such as creating inquirers and thinkers.

These are complex issues, and partly about students' lives well in the future. Therefore we introduce proxies – scores that are related to our real goals, and can be measured quantitatively. Sometimes these are chosen for convenience. It is harder to measure reflection and understanding than to rate word recognition, so word recognition can get a higher priority. Creativity, initiative and the PYP action component area are no less of a priority for being complex and hard to quantify.

Unfortunately, tests miss everything that is not on the tests. The higher the stakes on the test, the more items beyond the scope of simple measures are not covered, and children's potential outside of test areas is not realised. Other problems arise when testing is disconnected from learning processes. Results may show that, for example, students' mathematical literacy average is 78 on a certain scale. You may want to get to 81, but the raw numbers don't indicate how. Such tests are like measuring your resting pulse. It helps show how fit you are, but doesn't develop an exercise programme. Quantitative data does, however, have a very significant role in developing 'profound knowledge', which I will come to later.

Other forms of evaluation, such as rubrics and portfolios, cope better with complexity, and often are directly connected to units of teaching and learning. They help teachers make better judgement about the students and be accountable to them, rather than being de-professionalised into technicians implementing a preset programme.

There is one clear use of bureaucratic approaches. Seriously defective teaching is clearly measurable and needs to be prevented. Such poor quality does not predominate in most schools. There is a danger in basing quality around preventing such teaching. Energy goes into eliminating poor practice, rather than developing the best. One can end up with reliable and consistent mediocrity.

International schools often have high aspirations, far beyond consistent mediocrity. In addition, students may come from many different education systems and language backgrounds, needing a very individualised approach that takes account of their different needs. To excel in this environment, the PYP has avoided a bureaucratic approach. (Its precursor, the ISCP,[3] didn't produce complete scope and sequences.) Rather it encourages a deep reflection about the nature of learning.

Lofty ideas are important, but they don't necessarily guarantee quality, or answer comparisons with national curricula, which are often based more on discrete subject-based outcomes. They don't distinguish schools which carry out their ideals from those which don't. There are good indicators of quality, such as CIS accreditation and IB authorisation. Both of these are based on standards about process rather than educational outcomes. As quality is so significant, it is important to know how such models may work.

W Edwards Deming

It isn't only in education that a bureaucratic model has many shortcomings in providing not just acceptable performance, but high quality. Many of these were highlighted by the American statistician and management consultant W Edwards Deming. In the 1950s he went to Japan, bringing ideas that helped transform their car industry which, like much Japanese industry at the time, had a reputation for cheap but poorly-made products. The change was dramatic, with more reliable vehicles produced more efficiently. More recently, his ideas have influenced the Toyota Way,[4] the philosophy of which, along with 14 principles, have contributed to Toyota becoming arguably the leading car manufacturer today.

Deming advocated a shift in focus towards process, rather than the end result, with everyone in an enterprise involved in improving their part. The parallel in classrooms is concentrating on teaching and learning, rather than league tables of final results, with all the school community having an important role.

Deming argued that quality in complex situations needed *profound knowledge*.[5] This was more than the simple knowledge of procedures of Taylor's 'scientific management', but included understanding a systems approach; knowledge of variation; a theory of knowledge; and psychology. Applying Deming's quality approach to education, *everyone* needs to know the processes of teaching and learning in depth, and contribute to improvements, rather than relying on external experts and systems. Thus in the classroom, it is not only the teacher who should understand the situation and have useful insights, but teaching assistants, students, and anyone else involved regularly with learning.

Profound knowledge is equally important for leaders, who need direct and detailed understanding rather than a summary set of figures. Teachers and assistants will have a greater knowledge of students and ongoing teaching than a school hierarchy does, and so have knowledge to learn from. As the Toyota Way says, 'Go and see for yourself to thoroughly understand the situation'.[6] This expertise may be extended by looking closely at examples of student learning, such as portfolios and work samples. Research has its more powerful application at this level, as it can directly influence teaching. It can sensitise staff to particular issues, and has important evidence about what should work best. Reggio Emilia preschools provide an excellent model of such an approach through their use of documentation.[7]

Developing profound knowledge is a particular challenge for international schools with a high turnover of staff and students. It may be lost unless there are ways of capturing it, perhaps in curriculum maps and clear documents that new members of staff can use easily. It isn't easy to understand fully a complex curriculum and diverse school community.

Deming's 14 points

Deming captured much of his approach in his 14 Points.[8] These are superficially simple, but have deceptively deep implications. I have rearranged and grouped his points below with comments about their relevance to schools.

Constancy of purpose

1. Create constancy of purpose toward improvement of product and service, with the aim of becoming competitive and staying in business, and providing jobs.

Our constant aim is improvement of our main 'product and service', student learning. When we concentrate on student learning, parents are satisfied and schools remain financially secure as an important by-product. (The converse isn't always true.) More importantly, students are well-prepared for their futures.

Constant improvement

Improvement is already a large part of the life of many schools. For Deming, improvement should be a constant process (referred to in Japanese as *kaizen*).[9]

5. Improve constantly and forever the system of production and service, to improve quality and productivity, and thus constantly decrease cost.

The Toyota Way has a similar directive: 'Become a learning organization through relentless reflection and continuous improvement.'[10]

It is easy to say *constant improvement*, but it isn't simple to build it into the life of the school. An important phase is review and reflection, but this has to be *future-oriented*, aimed at changes where they are beneficial. It is possible to spend considerable time writing extensive reviews instead of planning improvement, and in writing elaborate action plans instead of taking action.

One way of keeping such a future-orientation is to review significant events directly after they have happened, when they are fresh in people's minds. Rather than seeking strengths and weaknesses, one can brainstorm *what went well*, and *how to do it better next time*. This focuses on acknowledging good work and suggesting productive changes, and one quickly has a list of improvements for the next time. This also avoids the danger of seeking to apportion blame for anything that didn't go well.

Constant improvement doesn't mean rushing headlong into frantic changes, enacting every possibility that arises. According to Toyota Way: 'Build a culture of stopping to fix problems, to get quality right the first time.'[11] This may mean undertaking fewer initiatives, but taking the time to do them all well. Chopping and changing initiatives means that much good work is lost.

Professional development

The importance of professional development is highlighted in two of Deming's points:

6. Institute training on the job.

13. Institute a vigorous program of education and self-improvement.

These points are quite self-explanatory, and reinforced by Toyota Way Part 10: 'Develop exceptional people and teams who follow your company's philosophy.'

Standards and objectives

Deming's eleventh point seems to run contrary to current educational practice, when many systems highlight expectations for test scores:

11. a) Eliminate work standards (quotas) on the factory floor. Substitute leadership.

    b) Eliminate management by objective. Eliminate management by numbers, numerical goals. Substitute leadership.

Much time is wasted if one stops teaching, planning and reflecting to undertake standardised tests and 'quality processes'. Even worse, students can loose valuable time to undertake forms of tests that aren't learning activities. Deming, along with the Toyota Way, abhors waste. The most precious resource in most schools seems to be time.

It isn't immediately evident where rigour comes from, without such standards. How do we avoid subjectivity? One possibility is Philips' concept of objectivity as being 'opened up to criticism'.[12] With open discussions, the more people who examine an area, the more objective the final view is, particularly when they have different backgrounds and perspectives. This may well include using numerical data. (Deming was a passionate statistician.) However, his purpose for statistics was to inform understanding, enabling continuous improvement, rather than as an end in themselves.

Ending management by objectives also doesn't mean abandoning consistency. The Toyota Way says that: 'Standardized tasks are the foundation for continuous improvement and employee empowerment.'[13] PYP schools can have templates for processes like parent conferences and portfolios. They can have full sets of unit planners and assessment tasks and rubrics. They can improve them every year. Their purpose is not to measure performance, but to increase quality.

Pride not fear

8. Drive out fear, so that everyone may work effectively for the company.

12. a) Remove barriers that rob the hourly worker of his right to pride of workmanship. The responsibility of supervisors must be changed from sheer numbers to quality.

    b) Remove barriers that rob people in management and in engineering of their right to pride of workmanship. This means, *inter alia*, abolishment of the annual or merit rating and of management by objective.

Fear may produce short-term activity, but in the long-term it demotivates. For a 'risk-taker' culture, students, teachers and administrators all need to trust and be trusted. Good teachers know the value of emphasising encouragement, not fault-finding, in keeping students focused, and students doing their best so that they can be proud of their achievements.

Such a culture of pride permeating a whole school leads to the best work from everyone in the school community. Pride in one's work is a deep and long-lasting intrinsic motivation that management by objectives and performance pay cannot provide, and provides an excellent context for teamwork and cooperation.

Teamwork

Collaboration is a key part of the PYP. It is sometimes limited to subsets of teachers, but Deming's work implies that it should connect the whole school, and that everyone is a change agent:

9. Break down barriers between departments. People in research, design, sales, and production must work as a team, to foresee problems of production and in use that may be encountered with the product or service.

14. Put everybody in the company to work to accomplish the transformation. The transformation is everybody's work.

This is a marked contrast to hierarchical approaches in which only one person is responsible for any item. It makes it harder to apportion blame, but easier to have a group sharing the pride of a job well done.

There are many time and organisational challenges in involving everyone, including specialists and teaching assistants. It also slows down decision-making, but as many people are involved in the process, they can implement decisions much more rapidly than when something is passed though a hierarchy. 'Make decisions slowly by consensus, thoroughly considering all options; implement decisions rapidly.'[14]

Deming's role for leadership was to help these teams be functional, not to take over their function. Managers act like coaches, developing the talents of workers and allowing them the freedom to fix problems. They develop the next round of leaders. According to the Toyota Way: 'Grow leaders who thoroughly understand the work, live the philosophy, and teach it to others.'[15]

Buzz words

10. Eliminate slogans, exhortations, and targets for the workforce asking for zero defects and new levels of productivity. Such exhortations only create adversarial relationships, as the bulk of the causes of low quality and low productivity belong to the system and thus lie beyond the power of the workforce.

Schools can be awash with these. However, Deming is not discouraging all phrases, but rather exhortations about items beyond one's control.

No inspections

2. Cease dependence on inspection to achieve quality. Eliminate the need for inspection on a mass basis by building quality into the product in the first place.

Thankfully, inspection is not part of CIS accreditation, and even OFSTED[16] has now adopted a self-reflection model because it is more effective for school improvement. Similarly, appraisal and professional growth plans in schools can be future-oriented, rather than inspecting existing teaching for faults. Time and energy are better invested in professional growth than in inspecting for a lack of growth.

Squelchers

Professor Richard Florida initially studied innovation by manufacturers, including the constant improvement systems implemented by automakers like Toyota.[17] He then moved on to research urban development, and developed a concept of the creative class.[18] He claimed that creativity and openness create higher rates of innovation and high-wage economic growth. Such creativity enables schools to be successful, and provides students with ways of working that will enable them to thrive as adults.

As he investigated how cities can develop a creative culture, he found people who undermined creativity, who he called *squelchers*. They preferred the conventional and diverted creative energy by blocking new ideas. Communities that didn't thrive tended to have as much creative energy as those that thrived, but they had a bigger quotient of squelchers.

Schools may have a few squelchers, some of whom are also passionate about education, but create obstructions to carrying out deeper quality processes. This often stems from a misplaced idea of what produces quality. Squelching, besides being a terrible model for children, makes it hard to sustain constant improvement, teamwork and a culture of pride.

Conclusions

International schools commonly strive for a great education, powerful learning that they can demonstrate to parents. However, this can't be left to chance. The curriculum is complex, and a diverse community places many demands on staff. In such a situation, a bureaucratic approach is not very effective, although there may be some squelchers who prefer it.

It is more effective to put time and energy into developing the features that produce genuine quality. This means working consistently towards our long-term purpose: developing students who fit the IB learner profile. It involves profound knowledge about learning, coming from professional development, and from using information about students' learning. It requires teamwork, involving the whole school community – everyone is responsible. Constant improvement should be embedded in the school and its curriculum processes, informed by reviewing careful observations about students' learning.

As we make these processes more explicit, and do them increasingly well, learning improves and we can be increasingly confident that we have excellent schools.

References

1. Liker, J. (2004): *The Toyota Way: 14 Management Principles from the World's Greatest Manufacturer.* New York, McGraw-Hill.

2. Drucker, P. (1974): *Management: Tasks, Responsibilities, Practices.* New York: Harper and Row.

3. The International Schools Curriculum Project (ISCP) evolved into the PYP when it was taken over by the International Baccalaureate Organization in 1997.

4. For more information on the Toyota Way, see Liker, J. (2004): *The Toyota Way: 14 Management Principles from the World's Greatest Manufacturer.* New York, McGraw-Hill.

5. Deming, W.E. (1993): *The New Economics for Industry, Government, Education.* Second edition. MIT Press, Cambridge, MA.

6. The Toyota Way, principle 12.

7. Edwards, C., Gandini, L., and Forman, G. (Eds) (1998): *The Hundred Languages of Children: The Reggio Emilia Approach Advanced Reflections.* Second Edition, Ablex Publishing Corporation, Norwood, NJ: Ablex.

8. Deming, W.E. (1983): *Out of the Crisis.* Cambridge, MA: MIT, pp23-24.

9. Liker, J. (2006): *The Toyota Way Fieldbook.* New York: McGraw-Hill.

10. The Toyota Way, principle 14.

11. The Toyota Way, principle 5.

12. Philips, D.C. (1989): Subjectivity and Objectivity: and objective inquiry, in Hammersley, M. (ed): *Educational Research: Current Issues, Volume 1.* London, Paul Chapman Publishing/The Open University, p70.

13. The Toyota Way, principle 6.

14. The Toyota Way, principle 13.

15. The Toyota Way, principle 9.

16. OFSTED, the Office for Standards in Education, initially used an imposed inspection model. Since 2005, it undertakes short inspections that emphasise school self-evaluation.

17. Kenny, M., and Florida, R. (1993): *Beyond Mass Production: The Japanese System and Its Transfer to the US.* Oxford: Oxford University Press.

18. Richard Florida wrote about the creative class in his books *The Rise of the Creative Class,* (Basic Books, 2002); *The Flight of the Creative Class,* (Harper Collins, 2004); and *Who's Your City* (Random House, 2008).

Afterword

Dennison J MacKinnon

In the foregoing volume, much has been written about the PYP and how it stands in a tradition of progressive, liberal education, which is determined to take forward the educational experiences of both children and adults at a time of great change in the world in which we live.

As one who was involved with the International Schools Curriculum Project (ISCP) from 1991 to 1997, when the ISCP handed over to the IB a dynamic, fast-evolving curriculum framework, which had been conceived and brought to birth in the world of international school education, it is perhaps apposite, over a decade later, to contribute a few observations about where the PYP is as the first decade of the 21st century draws towards its close, and where it is likely to be in, say, 2020.

In my article, entitled 'From ISCP to PYP: putting a curriculum framework based on solid research and best practice into international schools',[1] I outline the development of the ISCP from its early beginnings in 1990 to its handing over to the IB, as the PYP, in 1997. The article not only outlines the history of the ISCP; it also outlines the philosophical underpinnings of the programme and points out that it was originally developed for children being educated in international schools at that time.

My first reflection, over a decade later, has to be how much the PYP's 'customer' base has changed since the ISCP days. The ISCP was developed to meet the felt needs of international schools that were grappling, in the rapidly changing world of the early 1990s, with all sorts of issues, ranging, to say nothing of selection of curricular content, from appropriate pedagogy and assessment techniques, to the challenges and opportunities being presented by technology and advanced research into such things as how the brain works. It was believed by the ISCP pioneers that a new type of education was evidently needed in our international schools, one that would meet the challenges of the 21st century and which would lead to every teacher asking, every day: "Where and when will this child ever use what I am teaching her/him today?"

It is important to grasp that the great majority of the 106 schools that were members of the ISCP in 1997 were international schools. Only recently had a public school in the United States, Academy International, in Colorado Springs, come into membership and this was far from a 'regular' American public school. Most members of the project were international schools.

But, as one now peruses the lists of the hundreds of authorized PYP schools, it is interesting to note that 30% of these schools are in the United States and that an overwhelming majority of these schools are public schools. Public schools in other countries, including Australia and Canada, are also authorized by the IB to offer the PYP. The curriculum framework that the ISCP so skillfully designed for 'international school children', whilst still a powerful tool in such schools, has also evolved into an international curriculum for state schools in a number of countries. Public schools all over the world now deliver a curriculum that had originally been framed for children in another, very different, world.

And if something of the original zest and pragmatism of the project has, necessarily, been lost in its transition to becoming the PYP, for the IB is, of course, a large, bureaucratic organization, those who were originally involved can surely take some satisfaction from the fact that what began as a plan to develop a curriculum, or curriculum framework, for international schools, has now also developed into a fine international curriculum for schools, in use in good schools all over the world.

This of course has presented challenges to the IB, as schools which do not have control over either curriculum content or assessment strategies have sought to meld a cutting-edge programme with, in the United States for example, state standards and high stakes testing. There will, no doubt, continue to be a tension in such schools, as the differing requirements of the state and of the IB have to be considered and state mandates adhered to at the same time as IB standards are met. This will continue to be a challenge going forward, as schools seek to develop internationally-minded students and adults in public schools.

A second reflection has to do with the fact that the ISCP was years ahead of its time in much of what it thought and did, and in the questions which it asked, in the 1990s. By the early years of the 21st century, concepts such as inquiry, learning (as opposed to teaching), learning communities, authentic assessment, neuroeducation and third-culture kids were part of the language of the general educational community; but these were terms that were being used on a daily basis in the interactions of the members of the ISCP a decade earlier. It seems that if the IB is able to get the right balance, and encourage the crisp, sometimes revolutionary, thinking that marked the ISCP and has marked the PYP, the future could be bright indeed.

Given this, looking forward, there seems no doubt that if the PYP can continue to prove to be flexible, and true to its revolutionary beginnings, it could be a powerful force in education, particularly international education, for at least the next decade. The danger, of course, is that what began as an exercise could end as a formal organizational structure without either the strength or the wit to transform itself continually, renew itself and maintain a meaningful commitment to ongoing change.

But if the hard questions are continually asked, and meaningful change to the programme is made on a regular basis, there is no reason why a curriculum framework that binds together teachers from national and international schools all over the world should not continue to be a harbinger of all that is good in primary years education, constantly seeking out where progressive education might find a safe and secure home.

I am optimistic that there will continue to be powerful and talented successors to those people who, in the early 1990s, dared to think the unthinkable, think completely 'outside the box' and carve out, in the staid, complacent world of the international educational scene of the time, a rich curricular path. It will mean, in my view, that the 'hard questions' will have to continue to be asked and that the framework itself will need to change in response to changing needs and demands.

However, given the wealth of expertise that generally exists in international schools' faculties, and the increasing number of teachers in national schools who share the philosophical framework of inquiry that marks the true 'PYP educator', there is little doubt in my mind that the approaches to learning developed by the pioneers of yesteryear will continue to take the programme forward and that, no matter how much needed change there may be, the principles of genuine inquiry and of living with where the research takes one, will continue to ensure the success, growth and development of the programme well into the 21st century. People will, in my view, continue to 'take the PYP forward' within the PYP framework for many years to come.

Dennison J MacKinnon
St John, Barbados.

Reference

1. *Journal of Best Practices of IB Schools in North America and the Caribbean*, Volume 2, Issue 1, 2005, pp57-59.

Notes